# The Image of the Beast

## A Secret Empire

### or Freemasonry: a Subject of Prophecy

Richard Horton

Copyright © 2023 Ultimatum Editions.
All rights reserved.

Horton, Richard. The Image of the Beast: A Secret Empire; or, Freemasonry: A Subject of Prophecy. First published in 1871 (Syracuse, N.Y.: Wesleyan Print).

This book or any portion thereof may not be reproduced or used in any manner whatsoever without the express written permission of the publisher except for the use of brief quotations in a book review. The content of this book shall not constitute or be construed or deemed to reflect the opinion or expression of the publisher or editor.

ISBN 978-2-925369-02-8
Printed in the USA.

www.ultimatumeditions.com

# THE
# IMAGE OF THE BEAST

## A SECRET EMPIRE;

OR

# FREEMASONRY

A SUBJECT OF PROPHECY.

BY

REV. RICHARD HORTON.

# TABLE OF CONTENTS

PREFACE. ............................................................................ 1

CHAPTER I. ..................................................................... 15

CHAPTER II. .................................................................... 32

CHAPTER III. ................................................................... 43

CHAPTER IV. ................................................................... 53

CHAPTER V. ..................................................................... 61

CHAPTER VI. ................................................................... 71

CHAPTER VII. ................................................................ 101

CHAPTER VIII. .............................................................. 133

CHAPTER IX. ................................................................. 164

CHAPTER X. ................................................................... 186

CHAPTER XI. ................................................................. 199

CHAPTER XII. ................................................................ 212

CHAPTER XIII. .............................................................. 238

# PREFACE.

This work lays no claim to literary excellence; nor does it pretend to the most perfect arrangement of the subject. We deem the style of minor importance in comparison with the great idea which the author so boldly brings forward and so strongly defends. Upon the startling position herein taken, criticism is freely invited. It is believed that the time has arrived when the best interests of the Church and the stability of our Government, together with the present and future welfare of the race, imperatively demand this remarkable work. Prophecy unfulfilled is very difficult, if not impossible to be properly understood; but when God's people most need and can best profit by the warning and instruction contained in it, He raises up and inspires men to open the Book, and reveal those things which, for wise purposes, have been concealed from previous ages. Just at this period of the unblushing adultery of the Church with the world, having forbidden fellowship with the unfruitful works of darkness, and the temple of God has agreement with the temple of idols, we earnestly believe that God has raised up the author of this book, and endued him with Divine wisdom to fully explain and appropriately apply that portion of the Apocalypse, which has direct reference to our time, when the world is wondering after the Beast and his Image, and glorying in the possession of his mark. The contents of these pages seem more like an inspiration of the Almighty than the production of a human mind: more like the voice of God admonishing His apostate Church, than the warning utterances of human lips. The idea is, so far as known, entirely original, and with the application of the facts which support it, is for the first time offered to the public. We deem the argument quite unanswerable. The conviction is irresistible that if the "Image of the Beast" is not found in Freemasonry, it will be discovered in something exactly like it. As but one Image is described by the Revelator, and as Masonry is the only institution in the world that fulfills in every particular all the conditions of the Prophecy, we must inevitably conclude that the Image of the Roman Empire and the Secret anti-Christian Empire of Masonry are the very same. Gibbon, in writing the history of the Empire, wrote the history of the Beast; and Rebold, in writing the history of Freemasonry, wrote the history of the Image.

Should the reader wish to canvass the whole ground for his own satisfaction, we would recommend to him a careful examination of the XIIIth chapter of Revelation, with all the available light thrown upon it by commentators. Then read Gibbon's "Decline and Fall of the Roman Empire." Next take up Rebold's "History of Freemasonry," Mackey's "Masonic Lexicon," and Cross's "Masonic Chart," or any other approved manual of the Order, noticing, as opportunity offers, Masonic magazines and other literature of the Fraternity. Finally, or in connection, direct your attention to one or more of the following genuine expositions: Bernard's "Light on Masonry," Allyn's "Ritual," and Richardson's "Monitor." When God designs His people to understand His prophetic symbols, He places in their hands the means of discovering and applying them.

The Scriptures give us no ground to hope for the general conversion of the worshipers of the Image from their iniquity. Only the few who are sealed by the Holy Spirit unto redemption will heed the timely warning, while millions who have not the love of the truth, and are given over to believe a lie, will hasten on to their terrible and inevitable doom. The author's chief aim is to deter men from falling away into this great idolatry, and to point the Church of Christ to her most powerful, subtle and dangerous enemy in modern times. If the book meets with the hearty sanction of the Christian public, it will be revised and improved, and sent forth on its Divine mission to the world, in a more permanent form.

# THE TEXT.

## I.—THIRTEENTH CHAPTER OF REVELATION.

1. And I stood upon the sand of the sea, and saw a beast rise up out of the sea, having seven heads and ten horns, and upon his horns ten crowns, and upon his heads the name of blasphemy.
2. And the beast which I saw was like unto a leopard, and his feet were as the feet of a bear, and his mouth as the mouth of a lion, and the dragon gave him his power, and his seat, and great authority.
3. And I saw one of his heads, as it were, wounded to death; and his deadly wound was healed; and all the world wondered after the beast.
4. And they worshiped the dragon which gave power unto the beast: and they worshiped the beast, saying, Who is like unto the beast?—who is able to make war with him?
5. And there was given unto him a mouth speaking great things and blasphemies; and power was given unto him to continue forty and two months.

6. And he opened his mouth in blasphemy against God, to blaspheme his name and his tabernacle, and them that dwell in heaven.
7. And it was given unto him to make war with the Saints, and to overcome them: and power was given him over all kindreds, and tongues, and nations.
8. And all that dwell upon the earth shall worship him, whose names are not written in the book of life of the Lamb slain from the foundation of the world.
9. If any man have an ear, let him hear.
10. He that leads into captivity shall go into captivity, he that kills with the sword must be killed with the sword. Here is the patience and the faith of the saints.
11. And I beheld another beast coming up out of the earth; and he had two horns like a lamb, and he spake as a dragon.
12. And he exercises all the power of the first beast before him, and causes the earth and them which dwell therein to worship the first beast, whose deadly wound was healed.
13. And he does great wonders, so that he makes fire come down from heaven on the earth in the sight of men;
14. And deceives them that dwell on the earth by the means of those miracles which he had power to do

in the sight of the beast; saying to them that dwell on the earth, that they should make an image to the beast, which had the wound by a sword, and did live.

15. And he had power to give life unto the image of the beast, that the image of the beast should both speak, and cause that as many as would not worship the image of the beast should be killed.

16. And he caused all, both small and great, rich and poor, free and bond, to receive a mark in their right hand, or in their foreheads:

17. And that no man might buy or sell, save he that had the mark, or the name of the beast, or the number of his name.

18. Here is wisdom. Let him that has understanding count the number of the beast: for it is the number of a man; and his number is six hundred threescore and six.

# II—ANALYSIS OF THE SUBJECT.

## GENERAL DIVISIONS.

A. The Dragon. B. The First Beast. C. The Second Beast. D. The Image. E. The Worshipers.

### A.—THE DRAGON.

1. HIS NAME:—Dragon, Rev. xii: 3, 13, 17; xiii: 4; xvi: 13; xx: 2. Serpent, Rev. xii: 14, 15. Old Serpent, Rev. xii: 9; xx: 2. Devil, Rev. xii: 9, 12; xx: 2, 10. Satan, Rev. xii: 9; xx: 2. The Accuser of the Church, Rev. xii: 10.

2. PERSONAL CHARACTERISTICS:—He was great, Rev. xii: 3, 9. He was Red, Rev. xii: 3. He had Seven Heads and Ten Horns and Seven Crowns upon his Heads, Rev. xii: 3. He was Old, Rev. xii: 9; xx: 2. He was a Deceiver, Rev. xii: 9; xx: 8, 10. He was an Accuser of God's people, Rev. xii: 10. He had Great Wrath because his time was short, Rev. xii: 12. He had Power and Great Authority, Rev. xiii: 2.

3. HISTORICAL CIRCUMSTANCES:—He first appears as a Wonder in Heaven, Rev. xii: 3. His Tail drew the third part of the Stars of Heaven, and cast them to the Earth, Rev. xii: 4. He stood before the Woman, to devour her Child, Rev. xii: 4. He with his angels is engaged in War with with Michael and his angels and prevailed not, Rev xii: 7, 8. He and his angels were cast out of Heaven

into the Earth, Rev. xii: 8, 9. He deceives the whole World, Rev. xii: 9; xx: 8, 10. He accuses the Church before God, day and night, Rev. xii: 10. He is overcome by the Blood of the Lamb and the Testimony of the Saints, Rev. xii: 11. He has but a Short Time, Rev. xii: 12. He persecuted the Woman which brought forth the Man child, Rev. xii: 13. He cast Water out of his Mouth as a flood after the Woman to destroy her, Rev. xii: 15, 16. He was wroth with the Woman, and made War with the remnant of her Seed, Rev xii: 17. He gave his Power, Seat and great Authority to the First Beast, Rev. xiii: 2, 4. He is worshiped by the World, Rev. xiii: 4. An Unclean Spirit like a Frog comes out of his Mouth, Rev. xvi: 13. He is bound for a Thousand Years, and cast into the Bottomless Pit, Rev. xx: 2, 3. At the expiration of the thousand years he is loosed for a Little Season, Rev. xx: 3, 7. He again deceives the Nations and gathers them to Battle, Rev. xx: 8. He is finally cast into the Lake of Fire and Brimstone, to be tormented for ever and ever, Rev. xx: 10.

## B.—THE FIRST BEAST.

1. Referred to in Rev. xiii: 1, 2, 3, 4, 12, 14, 15, 17, 18; xv: 2; xvi: 2, 10, 13; xvii: 3, 7, 8, 11, 12, 13, 16, 17; xix: 20; xx: 4, 10.

2. PERSONAL CHARACTERISTICS:—He had Seven Heads and Ten Horns, Ten Crowns upon his Horns, and upon his Heads, the name of Blasphemy; he

was like a Leopard, with Feet like a Bear and a Mouth like a Lion, Rev. xiii: 1, 2. He was Incomparable in the sight of the World, Rev. xiii: 4. He was a Blasphemer, Rev. xiii: 5, 6. He possessed the Power and Authority of the Dragon over all People, Rev. xiii: 2, 4, 7. He was Scarlet-colored, and full of names of Blasphemy, Rev. xvii: 3. He was, and is not, and yet is, Rev xvii: 8, 11.

3. HISTORICAL CIRCUMSTANCES:—He rises up out of the Sea, Rev. xiii: 1. He received the Power, Seat, and great Authority of the Dragon, Rev. xiii: 2, 4. One of his heads was wounded unto death, and healed, Rev. xiii: 3, 12, 14. All the World wondered after and worshipped him, Rev. xiii: 3, 4, 8, 12. There was given unto him a Mouth speaking great things and Blasphemies, with which he blasphemed God and his Tabernacle, and them which dwell in Heaven, Rev xiii: 5, 6. He was to continue Forty-and-two Months, Rev. xiii: 5. It was given him to make War with the Saints, and to overcome them, Rev. xiii: 7. Power was given him over all Kindreds, Nations and Tongues, Rev. xiii: 7. All that dwell upon the Earth whose names are not written in the Book of Life, shall worship him, Rev. xiii: 8; xvii: 8. He leads into captivity, and shall go into captivity; he kills with the sword, aud he shall be killed with the sword, Rev. xiii: 10. The number of his Name is Six Hundred and Sixty-six, Rev. xiii: 18. The Redeemed gain the victory over him, Rev. xv: 2. The fifth Vial is poured out upon his Seat, and his

Kingdom is full of Darkness, Rev. xvi: 10. An Unclean Spirit, like a Frog, issues out of his Mouth, Rev. xvi: 13. He carries upon his Back the Great Whore, Rev. xvii: 3, 7. He shall ascend out of the Bottomless Pit and go into Perdition, Rev. xvii: 8, 11. He is the eighth King, and one of the seven, Rev. xvii: 11. The ten Kings give their Power and Kingdom unto him, Rev. xvii: 13, 17. He gathers his Armies to make War against the Lamb, Rev. xix: 19. He is taken, and cast alive into a Lake of Fire burning with Brimstone, Rev. xix: 20; xx: 10.

## C.—THE SECOND BEAST.

1. Referred to as the Beast in Rev. xiii: 11. As the False Prophet in Rev. xvi: 13; xix: 20; xx: 10.

2. PERSONAL CHARACTERISTICS:—He had Two Horns like a Lamb, Rev. xiii: 11. He spake as a Dragon, Rev. xiii: 11. He exercised all the Power of the First Beast, Rev. xiii: 12. He was a Deceiver, Rev. xiii: 14; xix: 20.

3. HISTORICAL CIRCUMSTANCES:—He came up out of the Earth, Rev. xiii: 11. He causes the Earth and them that dwell therein, to worship the First Beast, Rev. xiii: 12. He did great Wonders, and wrought Miracles, Rev. xiii: 13; xix: 20. He deceives them that dwell on the Earth, and the Worshipers of the Image, Rev. xiii: 14; xix: 20. His works were done in the presence of the First Beast, Rev. xiii: 14; xix: 20. He commanded them

that dwell on the Earth, to make an Image to the First Beast, Rev. xiii: 14. After the formation of the Image, he gave Life to it, and the power to Speak, and cause all who would not worship it to be killed, Rev. xiii: 15. He caused all the Worshipers of the First Beast and of his Image, to receive a Mark in their Right Hand and in their Foreheads; forbidding that any others should either buy or sell, Rev. xiii: 16, 17. An Unclean Spirit like a Frog, issues out of his Mouth, Rev. xvi: 13. He was taken and cast alive into a Lake burning with Fire and Brimstone, Rev. xix: 20; xx: 10.

## D.—THE IMAGE.

1. Referred to in Rev. xiii: 14, 15; xiv: 9, 11; xv: 2; xvi: 2; xix: 20; xx: 4.

2. PERSONAL CHARACTERISTICS:—It was the Image of the First Beast after his deadly wound was healed, Rev. xiii: 12, 14. It could Speak and enforce its own worship by the Death-penalty, Rev. xiii: 15.

3. HISTORICAL CIRCUMSTANCES:—It was made at the command of the Second Beast, by them that dwell on the Earth; Rev. xiii: 14. It received Life, the power to Speak and to cause as many as would not worship it to be killed, from the Second Beast, Rev. xiii: 15. It is worshiped separately, and in connection with the First Beast, by those whose names are not written in the Book of the Lamb, Rev. xiii: 8; xiv: 10, 1l; xvii: 8; xix: 20; xx: 4.

## E.—THE WORSHIPERS.

1. Referred to in Rev. xiii: 4, 8, 12, 14, 16; xiv: 9, 10, 11; xvi: 2, 10, 11; xvii: 3; xix: 20; xx: 15; zxi: 3.

2. PERSONAL CHARACTERISTICS:—They include the Earth and them that dwell therein, small and great, rich and poor, free and bond, whose names are not written in the Book of Life, Rev. xiii: 8, 12, 14, 16; xvii: 8. They were Blasphemers of God, Rev. xvi: 11.

3. HISTORICAL CIRCUMSTANCES:—They dwell upon the Earth, Rev. xiii: 8, 12, 14; xvii: 8. They worship the Dragon and the First Beast together, Rev. xviii: 4. They consider the First Beast as Incomparable, Rev. xiii: 4. They worship the First Beast alone, Rev. xiii: 8, 12; xvi: 2, 10; xvii: 8; xix: 20; xx: 4. Their names are not written in the Book of Life, Rev. xiii: 8; xvii: 8. They are caused to continue their worship of the First Beast by the command of the Second Beast, Rev. xiii: 12. They are deceived by the Miracles of the Second Beast, Rev. xiii: 14; xix: 20. They are commanded by the Second Beast to make an Image to the First Beast, Rev. xiii: 14. They are caused to receive by the Second Beast marks of the First Beast in their Right Hand and in their Foreheads, Rev. xiii: 16, 17; xiv: 9, 11; xv: 2; xvi: 2; xix: 20; xx: 4. They are the only ones that are permitted to buy and sell, Rev xiii: 17. They worship the First Beast and the Image in connection, Rev. xiv: 9, 11. They worship the Image alone, Rev. xviii: 15; xv: 2; xvi: 2; xix: 20; xx: 4. There fell a noisome and grievous sore upon

them, Rev. xvi: 2. They gnawed their tongues for pain, and blasphemed the God of heaven because of their pains and their sores, and repented not of their deeds, Rev. xvi: 11. They are not found standing upon the Sea of Glass, having the Harps of God and singing the Song of Moses and the Lamb, Rev. xv: 2, 3. They do not sit upon Thrones and reign with Christ a thousand years, Rev. xx: 4. They shall drink of the wine of the wrath of God, which is poured out without mixture into the cup of his indignation; and they shall be tormented with fire and brimstone in the presence of the holy angels, and in the presence of the Lamb; and the smoke of their torment ascends up forever and ever and they shall have no rest day nor night, Rev. xiv: 10, 11; xx: 15; xxi: 8.

The Revelation of Jesus Christ which God gave unto him to show unto his servants things which must shortly come to pass. Rev. i: 1.

If any man have an ear, let him hear. Rev. xiii: 9.

Here is wisdom. Let him that has understanding count the number of the beast; for it is the number of a man; and his number is six hundred threescore and six. Rev. xiii: 18.

Blessed is he that reads, and they that hear the words of this prophecy, and keep those things which are written therein; for the time is at hand. Rev. i: 3.

# THE IMAGE OF THE BEAST.

# CHAPTER I.

The book of Revelation was received by the early Church as a part of the sacred Canon of the New Testament. It was given by inspiration of God, and is prophetic in its character. The things which are contained in this Book were written by the apostle John as he saw and heard them, when he was in the isle of Patmos.

By the command of the Lord Jesus Christ, this Revelation was sent to the seven Churches of Asia. Rev. i: 2. Here is the clearest evidence that the seven Churches of Asia received the autograph copy of the Book of Revelation. Of all the Churches then existing these were the most suitable to be witnesses of the authenticity of the Book, that could be chosen; for they were acquainted with the apostle John both before and after he had written it, and were nearest to the place when it was written by him.

The voice of history declares that the Churches of Smyrna, Pergamos, Thyatira, Sardis, Philadelphia and Laodicea were planted and nourished by the apostle John. And he was the bishop of the Church at Ephesus after the death of the apostle Paul, who founded that Church. Such is the evidence which proves that the seven Churches were seven witnesses, unimpeachable and long-enduring witnesses, chosen by the Lord Jesus Christ, to attest the truth that the apostle John had written the Book of Revelation.

The voice of history which affirms that the seven Churches of Asia were intimately acquainted with the apostle John when he sent them the autograph copy of the Revelation, is fully sustained by the author of that Book, who says: "I, John, who also am your brother and companion in tribulation and in the kingdom and patience of Jesus Christ, was in the isle that is called Patmos." Rev. i: 9.

This declaration of John, that he was the brother and companion of the persons he addressed, could not have been believed by them for one moment if it had not been true; neither would they have received a book as a revelation from God, which had a lie upon its face. The fact that they did receive the Book as a Revelation from God, is proof that the declaration of John was true, and that the history which asserts the same things is also true.

Upon these mutually sustaining truths reposed the almost universal belief of the Church for two hundred years, that the first copies of the Book of Revelation were entrusted by the Lord and the apostle John to the care and fidelity of the seven Churches of Asia. These seven Golden Candlesticks, with Jesus in the midst of them, were not unfaithful to the trust, as the preservation of the Book and the confidence reposed in it by the primitive Church, will attest.

Justin Martyr, who resided for a time at Ephesus, about fifty years after the death of John, early enough to have seen the original writings and some of the original witnesses, says: "A man among us, whose name was John, one of the apostles of Christ, in a revelation which was made to him, prophesied that the believers in our Christ shall live a thousand years in Jerusalem." This quotation, partly drawn from the xxth chapter of Revelation, proves the existence of the Book at the time of Justin Martyr, and establishes the authorship of John.

These things are also attested by Irenæus, who says that the Revelation was written by the apostle John, and speaks of "the exact and ancient copies," probably alluding to the original writings in the possession of the seven Churches. The preservation of these copies by the seven Churches is further attested by the writings of Melitus, of Sardis, and Apollonius, of Ephesus. These ministers were the successors of the angels of those Churches who were addressed in the second and third chapters of the Book as we now express it. Melitus wrote a commentary on the Revelation about twenty years later than Justin Martyr, and Apollonius wrote about twenty-two years later still.

These facts show that the seven Churches of Asia preserved and esteemed the Revelation as a communication from God for about one hundred years after it was delivered to them. The strength of both the internal and external evidence of the authorship of John, and the agreement between the testimony of the Book itself and that of the witnesses to whom the Book was sent, gives a living basis to its history which nothing can destroy.

The apostolic origin of the Book of Revelation, the beauty and grandeur of its language and pictures, and the living force of its inspiration, caused it to be honored throughout the Roman Empire; though it employed symbols to represent that Empire which were witnesses of its crimes and prophecies of its destruction. It entered and remained in the Imperial City, though the burden of its prophecies concerning that city was its sins and its fall. It was preserved in cells and monasteries by Monks and Jesuits; and in the library of the Vatican, by the Popes, who could not conceal the fact that they were condemned by it; or that their own conduct was the moral and potent reason given why Rome should fall.

If the seven Churches of Asia are seven witnesses to the apostolic origin of the Book of Revelation, the ten kingdoms which now divide the Roman Empire are ten witnesses of its inspiration; for that Book foretold their coming, character and power, and the consequent decline and fall of the Imperial City, in prophetic language called, "that great city which reigns over the kings of the earth." Rome, at the time the prophecy was written, reigned over all the kings of Europe and Asia, from Spain to the borders of Persia. But the city of Rome no longer reigns over kings; they now reign over her. They have broken the unity of her empire; they have conquered her armies; they have destroyed her revenues, and all the emoluments of universal sway. In prophetic language, they have "made her desolate and naked, and eaten her flesh, and burned her with fire." This consuming process has been going on till the great city which once numbered its millions, is now reduced to the fraction of one; and that fraction not inhabiting the place where Rome formerly stood, has left the ancient city in massive ruins upon its seven hills. Nature herself is spreading the desolation foretold; for malaria and pestilence, from the Campagna of Rome and the Poutine marshes, are carrying sickness and death around the fallen metropolis of the world.

The keys of the Apocalypse are given into our hands in the nineteenth verse of the first chapter: "Write the things which thou have seen, and the things which are, and the things which shall be hereafter." "The things which are" were things of the then present, and the "things which shall be hereafter" were things of the then future, many of which are now past, and some still future. The things which John saw were representations of real objects and events, present and future. The seven golden candlesticks represented the seven Churches of Asia. These seven Churches were literal, and all that ever happened to them or was done by them were facts of history; hence John's visions symbolized real things and historical facts, "The things which are" were given to show the nature of "the things which shall be hereafter." "The things which are" were real things, and the things which shall be must also be real objects and literal facts. These keys being given by Him who holds the keys of death and hell, we are forced to believe that the symbols and representation of this Book, have a purely historic and real interpretation.

The Revelation presents a series of prophecies of institutions to arise and events to occur, which begins with the impending trials of the seven Churches, and extend to the end of time. When John, the last of the prophets, has written the last of this series between the beginning of the chain and the end of the world, there was neither space nor need for recording more. Any prophecy concerning this world, subsequent to the Apocalyptic series, must of necessity be false—a lie against the facts of the universe and Him who is their Author; and to take away one prophecy from this series, would break the chain and falsify the order of events foretold. To say that not one of these prophecies has yet been fulfilled, is to intimate that they are untrue. To admit that they have been fulfilled, but say that no man could tell what it was that fulfilled them, is to insinuate that they are useless, which is virtually to deny that they are given by inspiration of God. Impressed with the importance of this subject, commentators have searched out and recorded many proofs of the inspiration of this Book, by showing the faithful accomplishment of its predictions. Ministers of the early Church began to unite upon it as soon as its prophecies began to be unfolded in history, shortly after the death of its inspired author. Commentators of every age and many nationalities have continued from then till the present, as the prophetic symbols have been developed in the unrolling scroll of time to accumulate additional evidence of the Divine origin of the Book.

Seeing that the Roman Empire so manifestly fulfilled the prophecy of the ten-horned beast of Daniel and John, and that nothing else in any sense answered the requirements, produced a general agreement between Irenæus, Jerome, Newton, Taber, Scott, Clarke, Benson, Barnes and many other expositors, that the symbolic beast which our sinful world has worshiped so much was nothing more nor less than the Roman Empire; or, in other words, they beheld full and unmistakable evidence that the Roman Empire was the ten-horned beast.

Reader, if you believe from the mass of solid evidence poured out by the centuries and collected by the commentators, that the Roman Empire is the Beast, will you believe if an equal amount of evidence is produced, that Freemasonry is the Image of that Beast? It is but fair for us to expect you to believe it; or will you demand more evidence to prove the identity of Masonry and the Image than is required to establish that of the Empire and the Beast? And should we find more proof that Masonry is the Image than commentators have found in a search of eighteen hundred years that the Empire is the Beast, will you then believe it? Many do believe it now, and many more will ere long; for the prophecy of the Image of the Beast is being revealed in this our day, and the facts locked up and rooted in the symbol are bursting forth in the field of history before our eyes. By the general recognition and acceptance of this application of the Image, Freemasonry which was intended by authors and advocates to destroy Christianity, will be compelled to bear witness to its truth with voice and form as weird and strange as that of devils testifying to the divinity of Christ with whom they were at war.

Jesus Christ lived and died as a subject of the Roman Empire, and the history of His Church is so intimately connected with the history of that Empire that neither can be understood without a knowledge of both. In extent, duration and character, the Roman Empire is the most remarkable dominion in the annals of time. Diplomacy, wealth, intelligence and courage have always directed and sustained its armies. Its forces have sometimes lost a battle; but they never lost a war. Its history is better understood than that of any other government, because its historians are more intelligent, truthful and numerous than those of any other empire. And notwithstanding the present condition of that city which was once its capital, it is still the glory of all lands. This remarkable Empire has a double history; one natural, the other prophetic. The natural history was written by uninspired men after the data and facts which constitute it existed. The prophetic history was written by inspired men before such data and facts existed. The wonderfully accurate correspondence of the prophetic history of Rome, as indited by the Prophets, with the natural history of the Empire as recorded by the historians, is an incontrovertible evidence of the Divine origin of the prophetic history, the clearest proof of its Inspiration.

The prophet Daniel has given a short outline of prophetic history in the second chapter of his book. The metallic image of that chapter was the symbol of four great monarchies. It appeared in a dream to Nebuchadnezzar, who was the king of the first of these four great monarchies, and Daniel informed him that the gold, silver, brass, and iron which composed the great image, were four kingdoms; that the kingdom of Babylon was the first, for he was the head of gold; and that a second, third and fourth kIngdom of a like worldly nature should arise. He further explained that "the fourth kingdom shall be strong as iron; for as much as iron breaks in pieces and subdues all things, and as iron that breaks all these, shall it break in pieces and bruise." This terrible kingdom is the last earthly monarchy that shall ever exist or oppress mankind; for the kingdom of God shall break this kingdom of iron to pieces, and "stand forever." Daniel says that "in the days of these kings shall the God of heaven set up a kingdom which shall never be destroyed."

The natural history of nations attests the truthfulness of this prophetic outline. Four great monarchies have succeeded each other in the world, the Babylonian, Medo-Persian, Grecian and Roman. The last has the strength of iron and is the greatest of the four. And it is well-known that in the days of the kings of the fourth monarchy, in the reigns of Augustus and Tiberius Cæsar, Christ came to set up his kingdom. The prophetic history of these monarchies cannot be understood without some knowledge of their natural history. Their order, number and symbolic names are given in prophecy. In history we find the same order and number, but different names. The prophetic name of the Greek monarchy is, "a third kingdom of brass;" and "the fourth kingdom of iron" in prophecy, is called by men, the Roman Empire. The iron monarchy or Roman Empire, has been broken into ten parts or kingdoms, by the invasion of northern nations, and by subsequent additions and divisions, into very many; but in prophetic language they are still counted ten, because the latter are merely outgrowths of the former kingdoms. The Roman Empire, in this dismembered condition, is fitly represented by the two feet and the ten toes of the dream image, composed, as they were, of iron and clay, indicating a confederation "partly strong and partly broken." Here is full proof that all the divisions and outgrowths of the Roman Empire are the feet and toes of the metallic image.

The United States is an outgrowth of the Roman Empire, and therefore belongs to the feet and toes of the metallic image; for the United States were colonized by England, France, Spain and Germany, and it cannot be denied that these nations are kingdoms or principal divisions of the Roman Empire, once governed by Roman emperors, by Charlemagne and the Cæsars. The people of the United States belong to the kingdom of iron. They are Romans, if these States being peopled by Romans can prove it; or, if deriving their laws, religion, civilization, language and existence from the people of the Roman Empire can prove it; or, if being governed for a hundred years by the monarchs of the kingdoms of the Roman Empire can prove it. They are Romans, and there appears nothing to disprove this position but the fact that the governmental connection has been broken by the force of arms. But this governmental disruption has often happened before between the different parts of the Empire without impairing the vital relationship, and is no disproof, but a new proof of the connection; for, like the other parts, the United States is still subject to general laws of the Roman Empire, called the Law of Nature and the Law of Nations. The two feet and ten toes, partly iron, partly clay, partly strong, partly broken, are symbols of the unity and plurality of the Roman Empire, which, in being divided, has but multiplied itself by ten, making the former four great monarchies now number thirteen. Ten of these are that plurality in unity which constitutes the Roman Empire proper and complete.

When this last and mightiest of human empires shall have fulfilled its own prophetic history; when all things that oppose its dominion are broken in pieces and bruised, then shall it be broken by a kingdom mightier than itself. The kingdom of God shall break in pieces this tenfold monarchy of men. The kingdom of the stone shall strike and break in pieces the kingdom of iron, and shall itself become a mountain and fill the earth. But nothing can be destroyed till it first exists. The feet and toes of the metallic image could not be broken till after they were formed. The Roman Empire can not be broken in all its parts till all its parts, divisions, additions and outgrowths first have a being.

The head of the dream image is much older than its feet. The process of formation began first with the head of gold, and passing downward developed the breast of silver, the belly and thighs of brass, the legs of iron, and the feet and toes of iron and clay. The feet and toes are the last formed; yet they are the first broken by the stone; therefore, though the Roman Empire is two thousand years old, yet it is the last formed portion of that Empire that shall be first struck and broken by the kingdom of stone. As the United States is one of the youngest parts of the Roman Empire, may we not hope—have we not reason to believe that it will be the first struck, held and glorified by the kingdom of God. Instead of the United States being a government outside of the Roman Empire in prophetic sense, every other nation having a similar origin is included in the Imperial Confederation. At this day it encircles the whole earth, and everything that it has not broken it has bruised. It is, therefore, God's witness to the nations that the glory of the fifth kingdom is near.

If the question should arise in the mind of any reader, "who could have symbolized so many nations before their birth, and spoken of things that were not as though they were?" we would answer: these nations and empires so vast diverse and numerous, were named, described and numbered by the prophets of God; and the prophetic history of the metallic image by Daniel, is the most compendious ever written by man.

The prophecy concerning the four great monarchies of the world, and the kingdom of God, is deemed of such weighty importance that it is given the second time more fully and impressively in the seventh chapter of Daniel. The symbols are different, but in each case the four great monarchies are the same. Again the kingdom of Babylon is the first of these monarchies, for one of its kings is the head of gold, and the second prophecy dates from the first year of the reign of another; therefore the kingdom of Babylon is number one. This kingdom was overthrown by the Medes and Persians, number two. Their kingdom was next overthrown by Alexander and his Greek armies, whose consequent sovereignty is number three. The kingdom of the Greeks was finally conquered and incorporated by the Romans, number four.

According to the number and order of the symbols both in the second and seventh chapters of Daniel, the Roman Empire is the fourth universal monarchy, itself, in turn, destined to be destroyed by the kingdom of God. This, which is the fifth kingdom, in the second chapter, is represented as a stone rolling down the steep declivities of a mountain, and with great force smiting and breaking in pieces the feet and legs of iron, and grinding to powder every metal in the image, till the wind carries all away. This is further explained in the seventh chapter, that while the fourth monarchy makes war with the saints and overcomes them, the king of the fifth monarchy appears with the clouds of heaven in power and great glory. He sits as Judge between the contending parties and renders judgment against the fourth monarchy. All the thrones of Rome are "cast down" and the throneless Empire is given to the saints, who shall possess it forever—even forever and ever.

Four metals are the symbols of the four great monarchies in the second chapter. In the seventh chapter, four great beasts are the symbols of these same monarchies. According to the numbering of the angel, "the fourth beast shall be the fourth kingdom upon earth." Now, as the Roman Empire is the fourth kingdom, it is therefore the fourth beast; and as the fourth beast has "ten horns," (verse 7), therefore the Roman Empire is the ten-horned beast, and he may always be known by the number of his horns. The apostle John often beheld this beast and twice counted the number of his horns, (Rev, chapters xiii and xvii), and found them ten. No other number would correspond with the ten toes of the metallic image, and the ten parts into which the Roman Empire was broken by the sword of the northern nations. These parts could be clearly seen in the eighth century, under ten governments. They are the "ten horns (coming) out of the (fourth) kingdom," (verse 24), the ten kings that should arise.

Since the Roman Monarchy has passed into the horned state—since the beast has gotten his horns, the Russian Empire, which covers one-seventh part of the earth, the whole continent of America, and many other nations, have been added to the Roman dominion; but they have all grown out of the horns and not out of the head of the fourth beast. They are, therefore, massive branches of those tremendous horns which enables the fourth beast to fulfill the prophecy concerning himself, (verse 23.) "The fourth beast shall be the fourth kingdom upon earth, which shall be diverse from all kingdoms, and shall devour the whole earth, and shall tread it down and break it in pieces." It is vain to say that the "whole earth" which the beast was to devour simply means the Roman Empire proper and exclusive; for that would make the prophet say the beast should eat himself. With such an interpretation, the beast being the empire, he would be required to tread down and break his own flesh and horns in pieces. The true meaning evidently is, that he should employ three modes of destruction against the whole earth. He should obtain dominion over all the earth by devouring it—by treading it down and by breaking it in pieces. That part of the earth he devoured was his food, which, being assimilated by organic action, contributed to his nourishment and growth. The other two parts he has trodden under foot, or has broken or is breaking in pieces with his horns. When he has finished his work, he shall receive his doom from Him whose "throne is like the fiery flame, and his wheels as burning fire."

In early times the Roman Empire only devoured the nations that it conquered; but in later times, and in its horned state, it devoured its conquerors. The northern nations, from the banks of the Rhine to the borders of China, moved against the Empire for four hundred years. They dismembered it and entered the imperial city; but they never returned. They conquered their way into the throat of the beast, and were swallowed up, drawing many nations after them.

# CHAPTER II.

To the reader who examines with care what he reads, we have a few words to say, that such may the more easily understand what we believe, and what we have written.

We believe, that from what Freemasons call Freemasonry of the Middle Ages, have sprung all modern Masonic systems, rites and degrees, whether they be partly obsolete or worked in full. All "side degrees," and Androgynal Masonry, which admits women, and all the other secret societies of the world, existing among Christian nations, whether their professed object be murder or temperance; whether they be infidel as the Illuminati; political as the Know-nothings; ecclesiastical as the Jesuits; or judicial and punitive as the Inquisition; or whether their character be martial, social or frivolous, each of them bears some mark of the original, and all are always conducted under more or less modified Masonic forms, the inventions of Freemasons. They are all different forms of Masonry, yet preserving the same spirit in a greater or less degree.

Iluminism, which sought the overthrow of Christianity and all civil government, was a Masonic creation. While the highest Masonic authorities deny that it was Masonry, they acknowledge that men who became Freemasons made it; that they taught the three lower degrees of Masonry, and engrafted Illuminism upon them.

Adoptive Masonry, which has been the subject of so much scandal, is acknowledged by the "Masonic Lexicon," to be a creation of the highest Masonic body of France, the Grand Orient, which would not allow any but Masons to attend the Lodge of Adoption with the women. It is also maintained and published by Masonic historians, that the Jesuits created whole Masonic systems, and taught and spread them over Europe and the world; therefore the Jesuits were Freemasons.

The proof everywhere abounds that the Inquisition originated with and was conducted by Monks; and in Masonic history, the evidence is conclusive that at the same period the Monks were celebrating Masonic mysteries in their monasteries, and often were masters of Masonic lodges; therefore the Inquisitors were Freemasons. This Masonic testimony is greatly corroborated by the fact, that the Catholic Church has bestowed her titles and usages on Masonry, while Masonry in turn has left idolatry, secrecy, oaths and other indubitable marks of its influence on the Catholic Church, showing that the most intimate relation and harmony once existed between them. It is in this relation that we believe they both drank deeply of the blood of the martyrs.

Such are some of the reasons which support the opinion that all the secret institutions of the world have one common origin, whether they are institutions of the Catholic Church, or of the Mormon Church, which seems to be full of them, or of the Greek or Protestant Churches, or of the world outside the Christian pale. All are either Masonry, or some outgrowth of it, and collectively constitute the secret or invisible empire symbolized in prophecy by an image. For this reason, and for the sake of convenience, we have sometimes used the term Masonry, to express a generic idea, which includes the whole assemblage of secret institutions. As each new science imparts a new meaning to certain words which writers employ to express the principles peculiar to each, so Masonry, differing from every other system in its theology, morality and organic character, and the Scriptural symbols which refer to it, have added something new to the meaning of certain words which we have employed in delineating its character.

If it be clear that the secret societies of our day sprung from Masonry, it is still clearer that Speculative Masonry sprung from Operative Masonry; that is, the Freemasonry of today originated from an association of mechanics, which existed in the Roman Empire, and variously known as Colleges of Builders, Corporations of Builders, Operative Freemasons, etc. They were stone-masons and sculptors, who worked in stone and marble, and in the earlier days of the Empire, built theatres and heathen temples, and filled them with the images of their gods and heroes. In later times they built gothic structures for the Catholics. Speculative Masonry derives its name and religion from those stone-masons. Masonic lectures and rituals teem with references to them, and to the tools which they used in building. Pictures of these tools are given in the "Masonic Chart" for the guide of Freemasons. Thus the internal evidence is sufficient to prove that Speculative Masonry sprung from Operative Masonry, while Masonic historians affirm it, and none deny it. They say that originally it was a civil and religious institution, which celebrated the heathen mysteries of the worship of Bacchus, and belonged to the State; that afterwards Speculative Masonry sprung up in those civil and mechanical institutions of the Roman Empire; but it was neither civil in its character nor mechanical in its purposes. Yet it coexisted with the mechanical association till 1717, when it lost all connection with the mechanical arts and civil government of the Empire, though it continued to practice the heathen mysteries of the mechanics from whom it learned them. These mysteries, together with the working tools of the mechanics, mallet, chisel, square and compasses, etc., used as symbols, constitute the whole basis of Masonic teaching, religion and morality. For a description of these mysteries, see Dr. Clarke's Commentary on Luke, ix: 39, and Eph. v: 11, 12, where it may be seen that he believes the devil of the New Testament which Christ cast out, is the Masonic god, Bacchus; also that he used to enter into men when they were initiated into his mysteries, at the time they were taking the Masonic oaths. We have cited you to a description of the heathen mysteries by a Christian commentator and to his opinion of them. We will now give an exact quotation from a Freemason, containing his opinion and judgment that these heathen mysteries are continued in Masonic lodges to the present day, and are celebrated by the fictitious resurrection of Hiram Abiff from the grave, in the initiatory ceremonies of the Master Mason's degree.

"A very limited knowledge of the history of primitive worships and mysteries, is necessary to enable any person to recognize, in the Master Mason Hiram, the Osiris of the Egyptians; the Mithras of the Persians, the Bacchus of the Greeks, and the Atys of the Phrygians, of which those people celebrated the passion, death and resurrection, as Christians celebrate today that of Jesus Christ."—REBOLD, p. 392.

Christian reader, Freemasonry and Freemasons preach another Jesus whom you have not known, and another gospel which you have not received. Masonry mourns the murder of Hiram and Bacchus, but not of

Jesus of Nazareth, It celebrates the passion, death and resurrection of the son of Semele and not the Son of Mary. It attempts to teach the doctrine of man's resurrection and immortality, from the fiction and allegory of the resurrection of the widow's son, and not from the authentic records of the resurrection of the Son of God. The Freemason draws instruction and his hope of salvation from Masonic symbols, and not from the word and promises of God. The Masonic gospel is, therefore, a gospel according to mallets and chisels, and not according to Matthew and Mark. It supplants the truth and antagonizes all the loveliness of the Gospel of Christ. It removes the foundation of Christianity, and "if the foundation be removed, what can the righteous do?" It celebrates the heathen mysteries with heathens, and not the "mystery of Godliness" with Paul. If Masonry is not the "mystery of Godliness," is it not the "mystery of iniquity?" It does not acknowledge Christ; does it not, therefore, deny him? If Masons thus deny Him in the lodge and before its members, will not He deny them before His Father and the holy angels? It is a gospel axiom, that "whosoever denieth the Son, the same has not the Father." Is it not therefore true that Masonry has neither the Father nor the Son? If it has not, then do not Freemasons worship a false god, and not only celebrate heathen mysteries, which they acknowledge, but also worship a heathen god, which they in vain deny, since it is his secret worship that constitutes the Masonic mysteries? Is not their "Grand Architect" merely the heathen god of Architecture; or Bacchus, the god of the Builders, whose identity has been preserved by the oath-guarded secrecy of his worship, and the terror of its ancient and modern death-penalties? Is it not true, that the spirit of the Masonic lodge "confesses not that Jesus Christ is come in the flesh?" Is it not, therefore, "that spirit of anti-Christ, whereof ye have heard that it should come?" If it be true that Masonry confesses not the Son, and therefore has not the Father, is it not also true that "he is anti-Christ that denies the Father and the Son?" As Masonry is the only organic body which, in Christian countries, does this, is not this organic body, therefore, the anti-Christ that should come into the world? For this reason it seems clear to our mind that the writings of John contain two appellations which refer to the same thing; that the Image of his Revelation is the anti-Christ of his Epistles; and that both are Freemasonry.

The Savior of Christians told his people that he would send them another Comforter, the Holy Spirit, who should abide with them forever, and guide them into all truth. But no Freemasons, as such, has ever heard of Him; for, like Christ who sends Him, He is not acknowledged in a Masonic Lodge. No wonder, that not being guided by Him, the light that is in them is darkness; "and if the light that be in them be darkness, how great is that darkness." If such be the falsehood and delusion of Masonry, is it not reasonable to suppose that those who believe it, are such as have pleasure in unrighteousness, and receive not the love of the truth that they might be saved? For this reason, has not God sent them this strong delusion, that they should believe a lie that they all might be damned?

For the present we will leave the question unsettled, whether in Chapter or Templar Masonry, Jesus Christ is really acknowledged or only blasphemed. But all Masonic authority agrees with anti-Masonic opinion, that in the fundamental Freemasonry of the lodge, where the ancient mysteries are taught, and upon which the whole Masonic superstructure depends, no confession is made, that Jesus Christ has come in the flesh, and no recognition had of the Holy Spirit sent by him. Nor is such a recognition of either admitted. This fact requires no argument in proof of it. Hear what the beloved disciple who leaned on Jesus' bosom says in regard to such institutions, and to such men:

"For many deceivers are entered into the world who confess not that Jesus Christ has come in the flesh. This is a deceiver and an anti-Christ,—whosoever transgresses and abides not in the doctrine of Christ, has not God. If there come any unto you and bring not this doctrine, receive him not into your house, neither bid him God-speed; for he that bids him God-speed, is a partaker of his evil deeds."

We have given but a very condensed view of the origin and character of Speculative Freemasonry, in the extended sense in which we have used the appellation.

DEAR READER:—The object we have in view in writing this work, is to prove that Freemasonry is a subject of prophecy, and that the Church of God has been warned of its approach; that its character has been clearly delineated, and the magnitude of the danger flowing from it foretold. We have not, however, attempted to occupy all the ground. A field so vast requires more time than we command, and hands far stronger than our own.

Our position, we think, cannot seem unreasonable to reflecting minds, when we consider that Heaven has made the Church the object of its peculiar care in all ages. On the principle that "forewarned is forearmed," God has foretold the character of her coming trials. The prophecies which contain these warnings, are often accompanied by names, dates and places, involving the destiny of cities, nations and peoples that were to be the most intimately connected with the Church, and from which her chief dangers and trials were to come. For this reason the prophets have said far less about India and China than Palestine and Rome. Because the Roman Empire was destined, in the providence of God, to become the principal home of the Church for hundreds and thousands of years; therefore, the leading features of Roman history and character have been written out by the prophets beforehand.

Her institutions are all symbolized, so that, as often as the true Church should be subjected to great temptation, suffering and persecution, she might be duly warned of their approach, and know from which of these institutions her dangers and sufferings were to arise. It was so ordered by Providence, that these prophecies began to be better understood as they were more needed to sustain the fainting spirit of the suffering Church, proving to her members that God saw their sufferings, and would avenge their wrongs and reward their toils; that though they were neglected of few, He would answer their prayers, and what they said should stand. The best commentary upon these prophecies is the History of the Roman Empire. Should the belief be thought at all strange, that God has warned the Church of the approach and danger of Freemasonry, an institution which exists in every nation where the Church of God exists, differing in every respect from her, and yet often leaning on her bosom and dictating her policy, affecting society and civil government everywhere, and is acknowledged both by its friends and enemies, to be an institution of vast extent and power? In view of these things, is it not reasonable to suppose that a power so great as this is an empire, where everything else is so particularly noticed, and every other institution symbolized?

It is maintained by all standard commentators, those whose opinions are entitled to any weight, that the ten-horned Beast is the symbol of the Roman Empire and that the two-horned Beast is the symbol of the Roman Catholic Church. We propose to prove that the Image of the ten-horned Beast is the symbol of Freemasonry. We maintain that Freemasonry, as described by Freemasons and set forth in standard Masonic works, is proved, by the time and place of its birth, its character and history, to be the Image of the Beast. Such is the main position we have taken and will elucidate in the following pages.

We are aware that perfection is attained by improvements subsequently made on some original, and that here, no adventurous hand has ever gone before. It is true, some late writers have called Freemasonry the Beast, doubtless from the fact that they see his likeness in that institution; but do not seem to be aware that it is only his likeness which they see, and that his likeness is his image. We have drawn encouragement from the fact that the thinkers and writers of the age are approaching the discovery of a momentous truth, which brings warning and assistance to the endangered Church and the imperiled liberty of man. It cannot be expected that every question which may arise in a field so extended, can be answered in a space so limited; and it is too much to hope that no mistakes have been made on a subject so new. But it is earnestly believed, that the position we have taken is too strong to be false, and too true to be overthrown.

# CHAPTER III.

The thirteenth chapter of Revelation presents a diagram of prophetic symbols. These symbols are clearly distinguishable from each other. They differ from each other in their origin, and are symbols of different things. The first rises out of the sea; the second comes out of the earth; the third is made; all of them have individuality; each speaks and acts as a person. The first blasphemes God; the second persuades men; the third speaks, and causes that as many as will not worship it shall be killed. The first appears on the scene—the first in order of time; the second is second in order of time; the third is last in order of time. They are coexisting powers, with intimate mutual relations. The second exercises the power of the first; the third is made at the request of the second, and is the image of the first; it receives life from the second, and is worshiped in connection with the first; men being instigated by the second Beast to worship the first Beast, first directly, then indirectly through his Image. The first makes war, and is the symbol of civil government; he has seven heads and ten horns and ten crowns upon his horns, which are forms of government, kings and kingdoms. The second deceives men, and is the symbol of ecclesiastical power; he has two horns like a lamb, which seem like something of the nature of the Lamb of God and belonging to his kingdom. If the first and second Beasts are symbols of a first and second kind of government and people, then the Image or third symbol is the symbol of a third kind of government and people, intimately related to, and contemporaneously existing with the first and second kinds of government and people.

Let us now turn our attention to the thirteenth chapter of Revelation, and inquire what kingdom or power is there symbolized by an image—the Image of the Beast. Our great commentators are somewhat divided in opinion in regard to this symbol. Clarke, Benson and Scott think it is the Pope, while Albert Barnes believes it to be the renewed Roman Empire, after the time of the healing of the imperial head. These opinions have been generally followed in the smaller annotations, and by the Sabbath-school commentators.

We have one important advantage over these great and venerable men. There is more of this prophecy fulfilled in our day than there was in theirs. The thing symbolized proves its relation to the symbol when fully grown, by evidence which could not exist before; therefore the world is never certain of the meaning of a prophecy till after it is fulfilled; and, we believe, had some of these commentators ever had their attention called to Freemasonry and other such appendages to society, they never would have applied this symbol to the Pope, nor to the revived Empire. But how can anything be understood till it has lived long enough to manifest its true character? How can men clearly see that which is not clearly developed? How could the relations of Freemasonry to its symbol be proved before the evidence was complete? or how could Masonry be known before its history was written and its secrets fully revealed? The Image could not be recognized until it was perfected and exhibited. These facts will excuse them, but they cannot excuse us for making a false application of this symbol.

We believe that the Image of the Beast is the symbol of Freemasonry and its creations. Clarke, Benson and Scott believe it to be that of the Pope, and agree pretty well on the particulars; consequently they may be answered together. All believe that the ten-horned Beast is the symbol of civil government, and is the Roman Empire; that the two-horned Beast is the symbol of the Catholic Church, and is a Spiritual Empire, which they speak of as the Roman Hierarchy, or body of the Clergy, regular and secular; and that these Clergymen are the two horns of the second Beast. We are glad of their company and aid thus far. They saw clearly that which was matter-of-fact in their day. Other opinions defended by great names are also entertained concerning this prophecy, and we feel that unless we can give sufficient reasons for rejecting them all, as we must, public sentiment will not allow us to go any further. We proceed, then, to offer our arguments against those views which have been the most generally received.

*First:*—The Image could not be the Pope, because the Pope was a member of the Catholic Hierarchy, and an essential part of it, which constituted the two-horned Beast that "spake as a dragon." He cannot be the essential part of one Beast, its head, and the image of another, without greatly confusing the symbols. There is a very clear distinction in the inspired diagram of the chapter, between the second Beast and the Image of the first Beast; but there is no such distinction existing between the Pope and the Catholic Church; for the Pope is a member of the Church and head of the Hierarchy. But if this objection could be set aside, yet,

*Second:*—The Pope being but one man, could not fulfill the symbol; for at most, he could be but the image of an Emperor: whereas it requires an Empire to fulfill the symbol; for the first Beast was an Empire, or the symbol of one. It would take the Pope and the whole Catholic Church to make an Empire; but this Ecclesiastical Empire is the two-horned Beast, and cannot be the image of the ten-horned Beast. It destroys

CHAPTER III. | 47

the Ecclesiastical Beast, to make of him or his most essential part an image of the Civil Beast. If it were possible to set aside this objection also, still,

*Third:*—The Pope could not be the image, because he was made by a different class of men from those who made the Image. Who make the Pope? Benson and Scott answer: "The Cardinals create the Pope. He does not derive his dominion from hereditary right, nor from popular election, nor from regal appointment; but he is the creature of the Romish Clergy; yet being created by them, he is the object of their worship." Now the Pope is made by the Romish Clergy; but the men who have proved this, also say, that these same Clergymen are the two-horned Beast. Then the two-horned Beast, according to their own showing, and according to fact, is the power that makes the Pope. But it is very evident that the two-horned Beast is not the power that made the Image. It was made by "them that dwell on the earth," the party with whom the two-horned Beast was conversing when he said to them, that "they should make an image to the beast." Therefore, the Pope and the Image, being made by different parties, cannot be the same. Again, the two-horned Beast deceived the party that made the Image; consequently, the party that made the Pope, and the party that made the Image, can not be the same. The Image is something, therefore, that was not made either by the Clergy or the Pope, but is something to which they imparted life. If these commentators are right who believe that the Pope is the Image, then the fact that the Pope is an officer of the Church, and created by the Clergy of the Church, would prove that the two-horned Beast made the Image, which cannot be true, since he but requested others to make it. Dr Clarke, who has framed the strongest argument, extant to prove that the Pope is the Image, says that the regular and secular Clergy of the Catholic Church are the two horns of the second Beast. Did this Beast request his own horns to make the Image? This is not only absurd, but impossible; for those he requested to make the Image dwelt "on the earth," and not on his own head. Again,

*Fourth:*—The Pope was a long time in existence before the Image was made; for it was not made till after the imperial head of the first Beast was healed, it being the image of the beast whose deadly wound was healed. This healing took place in the year 800, when Charlemagne restored the Empire, and was crowned Emperor of the Romans by Pope Leo III. This proves, beyond controversy, that the Image could not have been made until after the year 800, and for reasons we will not now argue; we think not till after the year 1,000. It is evident that the Image is the image of the restored Empire, and not of ancient Rome. Now, who will presume to say that there was no Pope in being before the year

800 or 1,000? None. The Pope of Rome was acknowledged to be universal Bishop, by Phocas, the Emperor of the East, in year 606, four hundred, or at least two hundred years too soon to be the image of the beast whose deadly wound was healed. Therefore, the Pope is *not* the Image of the Beast.

It was to avoid the difficulties of the commentators just noticed, that perhaps compelled Albert Barnes to seek for the Image in the revived Civil Empire under Charlemagne. But in avoiding some of the errors of his predecessors, he seems to have fallen into others equally great; for failing to find the third Empire of the Diagram, he tries to make two out of the first; the one before the first Beast was wounded; the other after he was healed. This healed Beast, or revived Empire, he calls the Image. To Barnes and others who say the revived Empire was the Image, we answer, that cannot be; for,

*First:*—The Beast that was wounded, was the same that was healed; therefore, if the revived Empire was the Image, then the first Beast must have been his own image; must have been both the Beast and his image; for if it is only the image, then there is no beast; and if it be only the beast, then there is no image.

*Second:*—The revived Empire was the former Empire restored, and not the image of it. Or, if there were Emperors again in Rome, and the imperial Government was restored, then it was the imperial Government, and not the image of it.

*Third:*—The Image was something made in imitation of the restored Government, and could not have been made till after the restoration. The imperial head was healed before the Image was made; for the two-horned Beast "causes the earth and them that dwell therein to worship the first beast, whose deadly wound was healed,—saying to them that dwell on the earth, that they should make an image to the beast which had the wound by a sword, and *did live.*" So the head was healed, and the first Beast did live, when the second Beast conceived the idea of having them that dwell on the earth make the Image.

*Fourth:*—If the Government changed from a beast into an image, then it must subsequently have changed back again from an image into a beast; for long after the formation of the Image, the Lord and his armies took the first Beast prisoner together with the False Prophet, and cast both of them into the lake of fire.

*Fifth:*—The historian, Gibbon, in the "Decline and Fall," tells us that two-thirds of the Roman Empire, and the nations of Germany, were subject to Charlemagne. Now, if this be the Image, where is the Beast? It is nowhere to be found. Charlemagne, instead of healing the Beast, has destroyed it; for the Empire remained with his children to the fourth generation, and then was transferred to Germany, where the imperial head has mostly continued ever since. This would be inflicting a still more deadly wound than that caused by the sword of the Goths, Huns and Heruli, in 476. Sixty years later, the Goths were expelled, and the Beast began to throw out the seventh head. Three hundred and twenty-four years later, the imperial head was restored; but the injury inflicted on the Empire by Charlemagne, when he should have turned it into an image, has lasted a thousand years, and appears likely to continue to the end of time. But this position is still further refuted by the fact that:

*Sixth:*—When Christ afterwards comes to judge the nations, (Rev. xix: 20,) he does not find the Image; but the Beast and the False Prophet are still in their old place and at their old employment. Both are taken and cast alive into the lake of fire, burning with brimstone. Here we are satisfied to let the argument rest as conclusive; therefore, the revived Empire is *not* the Image of the Beast.

Although we may have cut through an army of eminent names, we are not free from difficulty. It is easier to reason with these men than to convince their servile followers. To the careful and honest student of the subject, it will appear evident that the Image is a separate and distinct Empire, symbolized by its own appropriate symbol, the Image. It could not be the

Catholic Church, or any of its departments; for it is symbolized in full by the second Beast with his two horns. It could not be the Civil Government, nor any of its modifications, for these are all symbolized by the first Beast with his seven heads and ten horns. Then what kind of government and people is the Image of the Beast intended to symbolize, and where are they to be found?

# CHAPTER IV.

We will now state some propositions which may be considered fundamental as a basis for future argument.

*First:*—The Image of the Beast, being made in imitation of civil and organized society, is itself an organization.

*Second:*—The pattern or model after which this organization was formed, was the ten-horned Beast with all his distinctive marks and characteristics.

*Third:*—The ten-horned Beast is the Roman Empire. On this, the body of commentators, ancient and modern, agree, from Irenæus of the second century, to Albert Barnes of the nineteenth. Catholic, as well as Protestant commentators are agreed on this. This opinion, based as it is on so much evidence, must be allowed to settle for the time being, the fact that the ten-horned Beast is the symbol and representation of, and therefore is, in prophecy, the Roman Empire.

*Fourth:*—If the ten-horned Beast be the Roman Empire, his image, or the organization symbolized by it, must be the likeness of the Roman Empire; for the Image was made in imitation of it.

*Fifth:*—If this organization be a likeness and imitation of the Roman Empire, it cannot be that Empire, but must be a distinct organization. This is abundantly proved by the description and character given of the Image; for after it becomes a living power, it enforces its own worship by laws or color of laws, and the death-penalty. It is said that "the image of the beast should both speak and cause that as many as would not worship the image of the beast, should be killed." This is sufficient to prove that the Image of the Beast is the symbol of an organization distinct from the Roman Empire, yet an imitation of it.

*Sixth:*—No small organic body of trifling power, limited extent and short duration, can be referred to in this prophecy. On the contrary, that organization, whether it be civil, ecclesiastical or artificial, being the image of a vast and powerful Empire, must itself be large and strong. This is proved by the fact that the Image of the Beast was a powerful and popular Idol, worshiped first in connection with the Beast, and finally independent of the Beast, and whose power was manifested in its ability to induce or compel idolatry, and to enforce it by the death-penalty on as many as would not worship it. When men worshiped at once the Beast and his Image, how vast the idolatry! It is said of the former, that "all that dwell on the earth shall worship him, whose names are not written in the book of life of the Lamb slain from the foundation of the world."

For these reasons, and others not now given, it is evident that the Image of the Beast is at once a wicked, long-lived, vastly extended and powerful organization, or an Empire of organizations, which men who are gone astray from God, are prone to worship. Such an organization is not, and cannot be any other than one of three kinds: namely, a political and civil organization, an ecclesiastical organization, or an artificial organization. By the first is meant a State, Kingdom or Empire; by the second, the Church or Churches; by the third, an Artificial Superstructure, built in imitation of Civil or Ecclesiastical Government, or of a mixed character, such as the Jesuits, Masons, Oddfellows and other secret societies of the world, or the aggregation of all, forming one vast Secret Empire or Artificial Government, with some kind of unity in principle, and derived from one common origin. Now we will proceed to show that the Image is not a civil nor ecclesiastical organization, but that it is an artificial one.

*First:*—If the Image had been a wicked and tyrannical civil government or nation, it would have been symbolized by a beast; for a beast, in prophetic style, is the symbol of tyrannical civil government. In this the great body of commentators are agreed. In prophetic style, the empires and kingdoms of the earth are beasts when separately mentioned. The Babylonian Empire is a beast; so are the Persian and Grecian Empires represented by beasts, and Rome appears in prophecy, four times as a beast. The last appears first as a beast with ten horns, the symbol of the fourth universal empire; (Dan. vii: 7;)—second, as a dragon with seven crowned heads and ten crownless horns; (Rev. xii: 3;)—third, as the beast with seven crownless Heads and ten crowned horns; (Rev. xiii: 1;)—and fourth, as a scarlet beast with seven heads and ten horns, carrying the great whore or Catholic City; (Rev. xvii: 3.) Now it is contrary to all the rules of interpretation and propriety, to say that the image of a beast symbolizes the same kind of government that a beast does. If the Beast be an Empire, the Image of that Beast is but the image of the same Empire, or an artificial government in which the image of that Empire inheres; for the Image was an idolatrous image, artificially made and appended to the Beast for the purpose of more universal and convenient worship.

*Second:*—It has been shown that the Image is a powerful organization, evidently an image Empire. But if it be an Empire of a civil and not an artificial character, then Rome being also an Empire of the same character, the two Empires could not have existed in the same place and at the same time. The Diagram clearly shows that the Image existed in the presence of the Beast.

CHAPTER IV. | 57

Rome was its birthplace; there it was proposed, planned and made; and at the time of its birth, it was the imperfectly developed image of the beast which had the wound by a sword and did live. They were, therefore both alive and existing together, and long afterwards multitudes worshiped the Beast and his Image in connection.

Thus we have shown that the Image of the Beast is not the Roman Empire nor any other Civil Government or nation. We shall now proceed to prove that it is not an ecclesiastical organization or the Church, neither in its pure nor corrupt state. If we shall do this, the conclusion becomes irresistible, that the Image of the Beast is an Artificial Organization or Mystic Empire; Freemasonry and its creations.

*First:*—It will never be said that the Image of the Beast is the pure Church of Christ, for the Image is a very corrupt thing. The pure Church is called, by the inspired writers, a Virgin, the Bride and the Lamb's Wife, and is always feminine. Whenever the true Church is symbolized, it is by a woman, and all her titles and symbols are feminine. The image of a masculine beast cannot be feminine, and the true Church, differing from it in her pure and feminine character, cannot be represented by the Image. The proofs of this are varied and abundant; but we need not stop to argue that which few or none will deny.

*Second:*—The Image of the Beast cannot be the corrupt Church; for that is distinctly symbolized by the two-horned Beast. This fact, so important to our purpose, is maintained by the great body of Protestant commentators, and is supported by at least three very good reasons. First, in some respects he looked like a lamb: second, he seemed to work miracles: third, he is called a false prophet, (Rev. xix: 20.) As he was a preacher and professed to work miracles, and had horns like a lamb, he must have been an ecclesiastical character and a professor of religion. And as he spake like a dragon and deceived men by his miracles, and is called a false prophet, he must be the symbol of the corrupt Church, and in prophetic style is the corrupt Church. Then if the two-horned Beast is the symbol of the corrupt Church, the image of the ten-horned Beast cannot be its symbol.

If the two-horned Beast is the symbol of an ecclesiastical organization, then the Image of the ten-horned Beast must be the symbol of a third organization; for it is clear that two organizations existed before the Image was made: namely, the Civil Government of Rome, and the Church. These two are said by commentators, to be Empires: the first, the Empire of the Civil Rulers, including the Pope as a Civil Ruler of a small part of the Italian Peninsula; and the second, the Spiritual Empire of the Pope, throughout all the boundary of the Civil Empire. This fact is clearly pointed out by commentators, and paraded as the solution of the great mystery of an "Empire within an Empire." But the depths of Satan will not be known till men perceive and acknowledge that a third Empire exists on the same territory: the mystery of iniquity will not be understood till men recognize a threefold Empire, all within the same geographical limits. All that seems necessary to this conclusion, is to prove that the ten-horned Beast, the two-horned Beast and the Image of the Beast existed together on Roman territory at the same time.

*First:*—This is clearly proved by the fact that the two-horned Beast wrought his miracles in the sight of the ten-horned Beast, and caused men to worship him. This shows that the ten-horned Beast and the two-horned Beast existed at the same time and place, and in each other's presence.

*Second:*—As these two Beasts take their rise in the same place, and after the rise of the second, dwell in each other's presence all their subsequent lives, and finally perish together, (Rev. xix: 20;) therefore the Empire of the Image which was made in the likeness of the first, at the command of the second, must exist contemporaneously with them, and in their very presence. The image was related to the first Beast as an idol to a false god, and the same men worshiped both the Beast and his Image. It received life of the second Beast, at whose request men made it, and it became a living Image. As it was an image of the ten-horned Beast and received life from the two-horned Beast, and was worshiped separately from, as well as in connection with the first Beast, it must have been distinct from both, and existed at the same time when, and place where, the two Beasts existed; hence, it was a third distinct Empire, co-existing with the other two; the first, Civil; the second, Ecclesiastical; and the third Artificial; the first two, ordained of God; the latter, made by man. This distinction is made clear in the Word of God itself.

We now believe it established that the Image is not the corrupt Church—much less can it be one of its officers; for an officer can be neither a beast nor the image of a beast, both the Beast and the Image being organizations. The Image of the Beast is the image of an Empire. Neither the Pope nor any one man, nor any unorganized number of men, can be the image of an Empire; and therefore can not be the Image of the Beast. If the image of a man is sculptured, we expect to see his features in it. If the picture of a family is taken, we expect to find all its members represented. And if the image of the Roman Empire is taken, we may expect to find in it the lineaments of the Empire—its titles, governors, governments, kings, priests, emperors, and the Pope himself, who was a civil ruler of an integrant part of the Empire, and spiritual lord of it all. The Pope cannot be the image of all these things and the image of himself too. But Freemasonry is the image of them all—is the Image of the Beast, and this image is nowhere else to be found.

# CHAPTER V.

The way is now open to prove that the Image of the Beast is an Empire of Secret Societies, and is entirely artificial in its character.

The artificial character of the Image may be seen by the different manner in which it makes its appearance in the world, from that in which the ten-horned Beast and the two-horned Beast appeared. The first Beast rises up out of the sea by a natural inherent power of his own, and appears on the earth in possession of natural life. The second Beast comes up out of the earth in possession of an inherent life and power peculiar to itself. These Beasts are not made by man; but they possess an inborn principle of life and motion, as all animated beings do, who derive their existence from God and Nature. But the Image derives its existence in a very different way, and from a far different source. It does not rise out of the sea, nor come up out of the earth; neither is it cast down out of heaven like the dragon. The thing was conceived and planned by the two-horned Beast, and made at his command by "them that dwell on the earth." It afterwards received life from its originator. It is very evident from these facts that the Image did not derive its existence from God or Nature; but that it is, in every sense of the word, an artificial superstructure made entirely by man.

If the government of the third or Image Empire is neither Church nor Civil government, it must be Artificial Government. If it be Artificial Government, then it must be the Artificial Secret Masonic Empire; for it alone has the third kind of government sought for, made in imitation of the first Empire, co-existing with the second, and is itself a third Empire, existing within the same limits as the other two. In order to find further proof that the Image is an Artificial Empire of Secret Societies, we proceed to an examination of the Diagram of the thirteenth chapter of Revelation.

The field on which the three Empires there symbolized were to act their parts, was the territory occupied by the Empire of Rome. This, in the time of Augustus Cæsar, spread itself from the Nile to the Rhine and Danube, and from the Euphrates to the Pillars of Hercules. But in the days when the Beast with the ten-crowned horns, and the Beast with the two horns, and the Image of the ten-horned Beast existed together on it, the territory was cut down on the east to the Adriatic Sea, and enlarged northward beyond the Danube. Although these Empires were not of equal age, yet they were all contemporary, and existed together on the same territory without destroying each other, but all acting in unholy harmony, The character and arrangement of the symbols prove this contemporaneous existence of these Empires, and their mutual relations. Now there are only three kinds of Empires that could each fill the boundary of the Roman territory at the same time without destruction to one or both of the others: the Civil Empire, the Ecclesiastical Empire, and the Secret Empire. These, and only these can explain the diagram and prophecy, and solve all difficulty. For the Empire of Civil Government—the Empire of Ecclesiastical Government, and the Empire of Masonic Government, could and did exist contemporaneously within the territorial limits of the Roman Empire, each Government extending itself throughout the Roman boundary, without either destroying any other; the Civil acting in frightful harmony with the Ecclesiastical, and Masonry with its creations, working in the dark in infernal harmony with both; therefore the civil, the ecclesiastical and the artificial governments adopted by Freemasonry, are the only three kinds of government that ever did or ever could exist harmoniously within the limits of the Roman Empire.

According to the inspired plan of this prophecy the Civil Government of the Empire is first symbolized; the second is the Ecclesiastical Government of the Empire; and the third and last symbolized is the Artificial Government of the Empire. For this latter purpose, Divine Wisdom selected a symbol which was itself artificial. An image is something that is artificially made in imitation of something natural, as the image of a man or a beast; hence the image of the natural civil government of the Empire, fitly symbolizes artificial government made in imitation of the civil government. It therefore seems clear that Masonry and its creations, with all their rites and degrees, forming the only artificial government on earth, and being, as will be shown hereafter, the *fac simile* of the Roman Empire, constitute the Artificial Empire that is symbolized and foretold by the Image of the Beast.

The next reason we shall bring forward to prove that the Image of the Beast is an artificial imitation of the Empire is, that the Word of Prophecy itself says so, either directly or indirectly. Does not the Word of God declare it is artificial, by declaring it to be an image?— for an image, being made by man, is always artificial. The argument may be stated thus:

1. The Image of the Beast is the image of the Roman Empire.
2. An image is an artificial imitation.
3. Therefore the Image of the Beast is an artificial imitation of the Roman Empire.

This imitation of the Empire is complete in secret societies, and in Freemasonry it is overwhelming. Whoever will define the word "image," and examine the relations of the object to the original, from which it is copied, will see that, whether it be an imitation, representation or similitude of any person or thing sculptured, drawn, painted or otherwise made visible to the sight; or whether it be a copy, a likeness, or an effigy, design is apparent in the imitation, and the work is the result of art; hence, Webster defines it: "The likeness of any thing to which Worship is paid; an idol." To this, we add the testimony of Richard Watson, who says: "An image, in a religious sense, is an artificial representation of some person or thing, used as an object of adoration, and is synonymous with idol."

The word "artificial" is used to distinguish things which human beings make, from those which originate from God and Nature. This distinction is kept up between the powers ordained of God and symbolized as corrupted by the two Beasts, and that created by man and symbolized by the Image. Roman Civil Government rises unaided from the sea. Roman Ecclesiastical Government comes up out of the earth, self-moved. Superfluous and blasphemous Artificial Government is made by them that dwell on the earth; and even its life and strength are artificial, for they are given it by the two-horned Beast.

In addition to the quotations made from Webster, Watson and the Scriptures, we give one from Barnes. "The word rendered 'image,' means properly, an image, effigy, figure, as an idol, image or figure. Here the meaning would seem to be, that in order to secure the acknowledgement of the beast, and the homage to be rendered to him, there was something like a statue made; or that John saw in vision such a representation; that is, such a state of things existed as if such a statue was made, and men were constrained to acknowledge it."

Though Barnes does not seem to make any special use of the truth he has stated, yet he has given the strength of his name and comment to the pivotal fact, that the Image is the statue or idolatrous image of the false god, the Beast, and bears the same relation to him, that the image of Baal does to the false god, Baal. Therefore, as he who bows the knee to the image of Baal, in that act worships both Baal and his Image; so also, he who bows the knee to the Image of the Beast, in that act worships both the Beast and his Image. This truth, freighted with tidings of measureless sorrow to so many thousands of our fellow-men, we do not intend to bring fully forward now. While a false god may be something in itself necessary and natural, as an empire, the ocean, sun, moon, etc., the statue or idol of a false god is always dispensable and artificial.

The Image of the Beast being the statue or idol of a false god, therefore it must be an artificial appendage to the false god. As that false god is an embodiment of civil society and government, therefore the Image of the Beast must be an artificial imitative appendage to civil society and government. To prove this, is to prove that Freemasonry is the Image of the Beast.

Now if men have drawn proof from the character of the ten-horned Beast, that it is the symbol of Civil Government, or an Empire, and from the character of the two-horned Beast, that it is the symbol of Ecclesiastical Government or the Catholic Church, what fair-minded man can object to us drawing proof from the character of the Image of the Beast, that it is the symbol of Artificial Government or Secretism? We think there can be none.

The artificial character of the Image and its organic insignificance in the sight of God, is further proved by the fact that it receives no judicial nor punitive attention or treatment at His hands. The sins of the Image are plainly recorded and are very great yet no judgment nor punishment of it is recorded as ever being inflicted on it organically; for God could not, without falsifying his own actions, and detracting from his dignity, treat with, or in any way acknowledge a Satanic creation. When God judges and punishes a man, or nation, or Church, it proves that they are subjects of Divine government and have a right to exist. But when he never tries to reform the Image, sends it no word of warning, and as an organization does not judge nor punish it, proof is conclusive that it is not ordained of God; that it has no organic relations to him, and therefore there is no validity nor binding power in its rules, laws, oaths, titles, officers, nor in its organic actions; and that it has no right even to exist.

Many may be ready to say: "If all this be true, then let them alone, for hell was not made for a Masonic lodge." Not quite so fast. Men are held individually accountable for their organic actions.

Although the worshipers of the Image are not organically punished, yet vindictive justice pursues them to their very altars, and inflicts upon them the severest punishment known to the Divine law. (See Rev. xiv: 9, 10, 11.)

From all that the Scriptures have said concerning it, the image is clearly an artificial appendage to the Beast, necessary for convenience in his worship, as an idol to a false god. Idolatry is punishable; for man, God's creature, commits it; but an idol is not, for the Scriptures say, "an idol is nothing in the world." In Rev. xix: 20, where the closing and grand climacteric scene is narrated, the Image is not punished, but is merely referred to as a grim and bloody phantasm, not recognizable in judicial proceedings. Far different the character and destiny of the corrupt Church and Civil Government! They had received their just and legitimate powers from God; were accountable to him for their exercise, and had abused them. They had encouraged and enforced idolatry, murder and blasphemy, and now their Judge is come. They propose to fight; but the Beast and False Prophet are taken and cast alive into the lake of fire burning with brimstone. We have now shown,

*First:*—That the Image is an Artificial Empire, by the fact that it did not rise out of the sea nor out of the earth, nor come into existence by any natural process, but was made by man.

*Second:*—There was a threefold Empire existing at one time on Roman territory, and of necessity, one of them must have been artificial.

*Third:*—The third Empire did not receive its life from God, but from the Pope and Catholic Clergy, and therefore its life is artificial.

*Fourth:*—It is said to be artificial in effect when it is said to be an image; for an image is artificial.

*Fifth:*—The same is proved when the Image is shown to be the statue or idol of the false god, the Beast; for the statue of a false god is always artificial.

*Sixth:*—It is not acknowledged as an ordained power by the Judge of all the earth.

Such are some of the reasons we advance to prove that the Image is an unauthorized artificial imitation of the Roman Government in the darkest days of its tyranny and corruption, and is a mere appendage to it; that it is a portable idol, in the language of Scripture; "made to the Beast," in order to perfect the system of idolatry, and for the convenience of the worshipers of the Beast, and that being made in close imitation of him, everything they loved or feared in the Beast might be found in his Image. This, in its application to Freemasonry, will be more fully explained in another place.

## CHAPTER VI.

We now proceed to show the date fixed by the prophecy, when the Image was made. The first thing to be ascertained is, when did the Beast himself appear? We answer:—about the time of the division of the Roman Empire into ten kingdoms. For the dragon, or second Scriptural symbol, the symbol of the power and unity of heathen Rome, is carried back out of sight in the retreat of years, to repose in that stormy sea from whence he had arisen, and had delivered up to his successor the Beast, his power, seat and great authority. But mark, there is a revolution of power visible on this first symbol of the prophetic Diagram. The crowns are transferred from the heads of the dragon to the horns of the Beast, which are the symbols of the ten kingdoms. These kingdoms were struggling together for birth about the year 400, and the deadly thrust of the barbaric sword was given in the year 476. The Beast received the wound in his sixth or imperial head, and Momyllus Augustulus was driven from the throne. The kings now hold, or soon seize their crowns, and the ten-horned Beast is the symbol of divided Rome. One hundred and thirty years after this, in the year 606, the Bishop of Rome is acknowledged to be universal Bishop or Pope, by Phocas, the Emperor of the East. Thus the two-horned Beast rises out of the earth and prospers till he exercises all the power of the Roman Empire, or "of the first beast before him." Their united power to persecute the saints, was to last twelve hundred and sixty years, and if 606 be the starting point, must have ended in 1866.

It was three hundred and twenty-four years after the Beast had received the wound, when the imperial form of government was restored to Rome. According to Gibbon and others, Charlemagne was crowned Emperor of the Romans in the year 800, by Pope Leo III, and thus the wound of the imperial head was healed. Now the division of the Roman Empire becomes a datum from which to start, and the well authenticated dates of the wound and healing of the imperial head, form the rock on which we build our argument.

*First:*—By reference to the thirteenth chapter of Revelation and twelfth verse, we find that the worship of the Beast did not commence till after the healing of his wound; therefore he was not worshiped till after the year 800.

*Second:*—It was still later when the Image was made; for the two-horned Beast had first deceived mankind by the miracles he had power to do in sight of the first Beast, before he said to them that dwell on the earth, that they should make an image to the Beast which had the wound by the sword and did live.

These arguments and these dates irresistibly prove that the Image was not made till after the year 800, and that we must go forward, but by no means are we at liberty to go back of this date in search of it. Neither can we go too far forward, for the following reason: The Pope exercised all the power of the first Beast, the Roman Empire, when the Image was made; but he does not now exercise that power. Some of the mighty States of the Empire have become Protestant, and the Catholic Princes no longer call him into the Politics of Europe. So small is his power in the European balance, that Garibaldi, an unsupported General with a small army, in 1866, shook the foundation of his throne and the triple crown upon his head; and his temporal power reels and totters to its fall. Indeed Rome has fallen with Paris in the Franco-Prussian War. For this reason we must turn back to an earlier date in search of the Image. It is now clear that between these two dates, 800 and 1866, the Image must have been made. Within this period we must look for its formation, and for some action of the two-horned Beast which gave life to it.

Now the question arises: Did Masonry exist in any of its modifications between the years 800 and 1866?

Masonic history answers, that it did exist in all its modifications within this period. Therefore Masonry had its existence in the right time to be the Image of the Beast. This was the time when the two-horned Beast exercised all the Power of the ten-horned Beast, or when the Catholic Church ruled the Roman Empire. All the modifications of Freemasonry now existing, took their rise in this period. There were at least fifty-seven Masonic systems, called Rites, that originated in this period. To these Rites were attached almost numberless Degrees; one Rite alone having ninety. All these Masonic systems, Rites and Degrees, together with many of the Secret Societies of Masonic creation, that do not bear the appellation of Freemasonry, were created within this period. Knight Templar Masonry and other societies which profess to have originated in the Crusades, were all within this period. The Crusades began in the eleventh century and ended in the thirteenth. The Jesuits came into existence in 1538. The present existing system of Speculative Masonry was not perfected until 1717, and we think not even then; for most of the Freemasonry of the higher degrees, which belong to the Masonic systems of our day, was not created and practiced till after 1717. Rebold tells us that a few of the higher Degrees were created by modern Jews; others by the partisans of the Stuarts, in favor of the Catholic religion and monarchy; and the rest of them sprung from the Jesuit College near Paris, and all before the close of the eighteenth century, when the Masonic system was fully grown; for Freemasons after that time began to combine and lessen the number of their Rites and Degrees; therefore, the Freemasonry of 1717, with all that has since been added to it, and all of its own kind previously existing, originated within this period; that is to say, all that Freemasons call Speculative Freemasonry, originated, grew, and was perfected between the ninth and the close of the eighteenth century, the proper period to fulfill the prophecy and to be the Image of the Beast. Within those nine hundred years the Roman Catholic Church exercised all the power of the first Beast, her Pope disposing of the crowns and thrones of Europe.

If Speculative Freemasonry is the Image of the Beast, then those Masons who have written its history, have written the history of the Image. One of them says it originated by taking the Catholic Priests into the Civil and Mechanical Associations of Builders or Artists. We quote from Mackey's "Masonic Lexicon," page 496:

"Freemasons were originally all operative; but the Artizans of that period were not educated men, and they were compelled to seek among the Clergy, the only men of learning, for those whose wisdom might contrive, and whose cultivated taste might adorn the plans which they by their practical skill were to carry into effect; hence the germ of Speculative Freemasonry, which once dividing the character of the Fraternity with the Operative, now completely occupies it, to the entire exclusion of the latter." [4]

It will be seen by this and other history, that Speculative Masonry originated by taking the Catholic Clergy into the worship and fellowship of a secret society of heathen mechanics, whose god was the Dionysius of the Greek Architects and the Bacchus of the Italians. The marks of the god were made with the working tools of the Architects, and the myths and mysteries of his religion were illustrated by them. Thus the germ of Speculative Masonry was formed by teaching the Catholic Clergy the religion of a false god without a knowledge of the trade peculiar to the fraternity that worshiped him. The germ of Speculative Masonry thus formed, "once dividing the character of the fraternity with the Operative, now completely occupies it, to the entire exclusion of the latter."

According to the Masonic account of the origin of Speculative Masonry, it was made by heathens in the Middle Ages, and received life from the Catholics. In Scripture, these heathens are spoken of as "them that dwell on the earth," who made the Image of the Beast, and the Catholics, as the two-horned Beast that gave life to it. Those Freemasons who have written the history of the Image, have given us more evidence of these things than we have time or space to record, and more proof that it received life from the Catholic Church than we want or need to employ.

We have already quoted from the writings of Mackey, an American Freemason of high authority. We now quote from Rebold, the greatest Masonic historian of France, page 74:

"In the eleventh century we find them again in France, where they are known under the name of Brother Masons and Brother Bridgers, and sometimes, also, under that of Freemasons, employed and directed almost exclusively by the religious orders. The Abbots and Prelates held it an honor to enter into membership with the fraternity and to participate in their secrets, and thus greatly promoted the stability and consideration accorded to the institution."

The Clergy held it an honor to enter into membership with the Fraternity. This honor was obtained at the frightful cost of swearing allegiance to the throne of Bacchus, and henceforth being doomed to worship at the altar of the Lord by day and at the altar of Bacchus by night. The Christianity of those days was thus so mixed with heathen rites, mysteries, secrecy, pageantry and idolatry, that the Catholic Church looked about as much like Freemasonry half converted to Christianity, as Christianity half converted to Freemasonry. Speculative Masonry derives the germ of its existence from the apostacy of the Catholic Clergy, in a period of general relapse of the Empire into heathenism. These Clergymen brought into Masonry the influence, power, intelligence and other life-giving forces of the Church, or in the language of Rebold, "stability and consideration," just as the fallen ministers of our day, following their example, give stability and character to the Masonic institution, by uniting with, and defending it.

Again, Albert Mackey informs us that the Knight Templar Freemasonry of the Crusades, was composed of "Nobles, Priests and serving brethren," and that "in 1128, they received a rule or system of regulations from the Pope." "The second class, or the Priests, were not originally a part of the order; but by the Bull *omne datum optimum*, it was ordained that they might be admitted."

Reader, mark the points already proved by these quotations. First, the admission of the Catholic Priests into a heathen mechanical association, originated Speculative Freemasonry. Second, their presence gave to the institution, stability and consideration. Third, the Pope asked for the admission of these Priests, or rather demanded their admission by the loud roaring of a Papal Bull.

In the Scriptural account of the origin of the Image of the Beast, the Catholic Church is represented as requesting a party of men dwelling on the earth, to make the Image. In the history before us, Speculative Freemasonry originates in the request of the Catholic Church, through her Pope, that her Priests should be admitted into a secret society of the earth, in no way related to Christianity, but which was a pagan and mechanical institution of the Roman Empire. In the Scriptures, the two-horned Beast authoritatively says to them that dwell on the earth, that they should make the Image. In the history, the Pope authoritatively ordains or requests a heathen society to make Speculative Freemasonry by admitting Priests.

The Scripture represents the Catholics as giving life to the Image. The history represents them as giving stability and consideration to the Masonic institution. Were not the Image of the Beast and Speculative Freemasonry made and quickened in the same way and by the same parties? Candid reader, are they not the same?

After the germ of Speculative Masonry was formed, there were two distinct sets of principles in the Masonic institution: the operative and the speculative principles. There were also two distinct classes of individuals in the institution: the operative and speculative membership. The former, each day, worked on at building, as before. The latter, also as formerly, ministered at the altar and table of the Lord. Then, at the full of the moon, they all met again at night, and worshiped the same heathen deity; while each member took upon himself the Eleusinian oaths and death-penalties necessary to the secret worship of that god. There now seemed to be an agreement between the temple of God and idols, and he that believed had some part with infidels. The love of the Priests was soon reciprocated by the heathen membership. Some of them joined the Church, and had a fair opportunity to partake, first of the cup of the Lord, and then of the cup of devils; or first, to celebrate the passion and death of Bacchus, murdered by the Titans, in the mystery; and then the passion and death of Christ, in the Mass, or of Hiram Abiff, the Jewish substitute for Bacchus, and whose fictitious passion and death is still celebrated in the third degree of Masonry. The Church now learns the power and advantages of oath-bound secrecy and adopts the secret manner of the Bacchanalian mysteries, and the Lodge adopts the titles of the Church and is ruled by the Priests.

Such is the origin and character of Speculative Masonry, or the Image of the Beast. But Masonic history must be examined before the reader can fully see that the Catholic Church long continued to give it life, by pouring into it her honors, wealth and membership, including the Catholic Nobility and Kings, besides the favoring Papal Bulls and civil legislation. Rebold, on page 50 of his history, gives a remarkable instance of the latter kind by Pope Benedict, who gave to the Masonic Corporations, special diplomas.

"These diplomas made them free of all local laws, all royal edicts, all municipal regulations, and every other obligation to which the other inhabitants of the country had to submit, thus rendering the title by which they were known, of Free Corporations, peculiarly appropriate. In addition to this freedom, these diplomas conceded to them the right of communicating directly with the Pope, of fixing the amount of their own salaries or wages, and of regulating in their general assemblies, all subjects appertaining to their interior government. All artists and artisans who were not members of these Corporations, were interdicted from every act which would in anywise interfere with the work of the Builders; and all Sovereign Rulers were commanded, as they dreaded the thunders of the Church, to suppress with the strong arm of their power, any combination of such artists and artisans as might rebel against this provision."

These diplomas which they received from the two-horned Beast, elevated all the members of the Masonic institution, in point of freedom and advantage, above all the rest of mankind; and these advantages were bestowed alike on the operative builders and the speculative members; the latter sometimes being both artisans and priests. This frightful and pernicious advantage, never before given to man, of being placed above the reach of all human law "and every other obligation to which the other inhabitants of the country had to submit," must have been more particularly designed for the benefit of the Priests and speculative membership who controlled the institution in the interests of the Roman Catholic Church, than for the operatives who did nothing but cut stone and build houses, following the trade peculiar to their god.

There were three or four different principles in the Masonic institution of those days: the operative, the speculative, the religious and the mixed. It was this complex institution that was placed above the reach of human law, while the law that could not control it was forced to defend it. Upon examination, therefore, we find that the Bacchanalian religion of Freemasonry was established by a decree of the Pope. The inherent constitutional tendency of modern Masonry to resist and foil the legitimate operations of human law, has naturally descended from these Papal diplomas. The germ of everything detestable or dangerous in Masonry, may be found in these diplomas; and all the infliction of wrongs upon society, of which Masons are guilty, is but the assertion of their ancient privileges.

Reader, did not Masonry receive life from the two-horned Beast, and is it not, therefore, the Image? The evidence in this case is threefold. First, the fact that diplomas conferring extraordinary privileges on Masonry, were issued by the Pope. Second, the heathen Bacchanalian religion established by them, continues to be the religion of Freemasonry to this day, and is easily recognized by its secret worship, mysteries, oaths and death-penalties, the characteristics of the worship of Bacchus and Ceres, as given by the Greek and Roman historians. Third, the fact that the characteristics of the gifts bestowed by the diplomas, are the characteristics of Freemasonry today. These diplomas having produced character, must have been a life-giving force to the institution.

Although Masonry received stability and consideration from the Catholic Priesthood as early as the eleventh century,—and though the Masonic Catholics, called Jesuits, who greatly enlarged, and for a time controlled the Freemasonry of the world, were sustained by a Papal Bull as late as the sixteenth century, yet the fourteenth century when these diplomas were issued, was the period more than any other when it received organic life. At this period also, the power of the two-horned Beast had reached its climacteric, and it is in perfect harmony with the prophecy, that at this time his breath should give life to the Image. For this act was to be performed when the two-horned Beast exercised all the power of the ten-horned Beast before him; or in other words, when the Roman Catholic Church exercised all the power which belonged to the Civil Government of the Roman Empire. The Church and Popes never so completely and corruptedly ruled the Empire as in the fourteenth century. Dr. Clarke says:

> "The plenitude of Papal power was not confined to what was spiritual. The Romish Bishops dethroned monarchs, disposed of crowns,

absolved subjects from the obedience due to their sovereigns, and laid kingdoms under interdicts. There was not a State in Europe which had not been disquieted by their ambition; there was not a throne which they had not shaken, nor a prince that did not tremble at their presence. The point of time in which the Romish Bishops attained their highest elevation of authority, was about the commencement of the fourteenth century."

Reader, is not the Image of Prophecy the Masonry of history? Are not the place and characters concerned in the origin of each, the same as those concerned in the origin of the other? Are not the parties concerned the same, and their actions whether distinct or complex? Do not dates synchronize, and history and prophecy harmonize in such a manner as to prove they are one?

It has been proved by quotations from Mackey and Rebold, that the germ of Speculative Masonry, a secret society that never appeared on earth before, was formed in the Middle Ages, by receiving the Catholic Priests into the Operative Lodges or the incorporated Colleges of the Builders of the Roman Empire, an institution of the State. The same thing is stated in stronger language by Rebold, in his Preface.

"B. Clavel, it is true, mentions the Colleges of Roman Architects; but always pre-occupied in common with his predecessors in seeking a remoter origin for Freemasonry in the mysteries of the East, he fails to perceive that it was precisely within these Colleges that the birth of Freemasonry took place. * * * The authors who pretend, and their number is very great, that Masonry originated at the construction of Solomon's Temple, are led into this error by the numerous allusions to that construction, which have place in the Lodges of today."

In regard to the birth of Speculative Freemasonry, this historian is sustained by the Freemasonry of France; for Du Planty, M. D., Auguste Humberte and B. Limeth, three Worshipful Masters who examined Rebold's History say, that

"Brother Rebold has taken hold of Freemasonry at its birth, and followed its growth and extension through its career from nation to nation and from century to century, and supports his every statement with facts, dates and names, and the edifices and monuments of antiquity."

This testimony to the true origin of Freemasonry comes from an enlightened writer of France,—a country where both Operative and Speculative Masonry had existed. His account of the birth of Speculative Masonry is sustained by a committee of three Worshipful Masters, near Paris, the capital of France. Thus we have a double assurance of its truth, and yet there is another. Those Worshipful Masters not only testify as historians and as men, but, in their own language, "with our hands as Freemasons, upon our hearts;" or in other words under the oaths and death-penalties of the Most Excellent Master and Fellow Craft Degrees. As Masonry, according to its obligations, may be false to all else, yet may not be false to itself, therefore we have the inside testimony of Masonry to these things, under the sanction of its obligations. Let no Freemason deny it. The writer having also examined the subject, believes that these Masons have told the truth in this matter.

Not only has the germinal formation and subsequent birth of Masonry taken place within the Roman Corporations of Operatives, but it must have attained to considerable magnitude in 1649, when it made new degrees, raised Charles II to the throne, and restored monarchy to England; and must have been quite strong at the close of the seventeenth century, when it took an active part in politics, wars and revolution. These are not the actions of Operative, but of Speculative Masonry; hence Rebold says, pages 54-5 and 311:

"During the troubles which desolated England about the middle of the seventeenth century, and after the death of Charles I in 1649, the Masonic Corporations of England, and more particularly those of Scotland, labored in secret for the re-establishment of the throne destroyed by Cromwell, and for this purpose they instituted many degrees hitherto unknown, and totally foreign to the spirit and nature of Freemasonry, and which, in fact, gave to this time-honored institution a character entirely political. The discussions to which this country was a prey, had already produced a separation between the Operative and Accepted Masons. The latter were honorary members, who, according to long-established usage, had been accepted into the Society for the advantage their generally influential position in the country might effect. But this very position made them at this time very naturally the adherents of the throne and the strong supporters of Charles II, who, during his exile, was received as an Accepted Mason by their election, and in consequence of the benefits he received from the Society, gave to Masonry the title of

'Royal Art,' because it was mainly by its instrumentality that he was raised to the throne and monarchy restored to England. * \* * The close of the seventeenth century, in consequence of the active part taken by the Fraternity in politics, wars and revolution, saw them scattered, their Lodges dissolved."

By the aid of these writers, the Scriptures and ancient history, we are enabled to understand the nature of Freemasonry and lift the darkness from its birth. Masonry is not the mysteries of Osiris, Eleusis or Ceres, nor Bacchus, nor Solomon. Nor is it the Operative Builders of the Roman Empire, called Colleges, which Numa Pompilius, the Lawgiver of Rome, instituted when he formed the different tradesmen of the city into different societies, and Bacchus was installed god of the Builders. But Masonry was born within these Colleges between the feet of the Operative Lodges. His mother was a heathen, and his father a Catholic Priest. He embraced the religion of his mother, who taught him the myths and mysteries of Eleusis or Ceres, and Bacchus. His father being a Priest, would not allow him to work. His mother permitted him to play with the tools of the stone-masons and builders, and make marks of the Beast among whose institutions he was born. His father's Scriptural name is *"The Man of Sin;"* his own name in

CHAPTER VI. | 89

Scripture is the "IMAGE OF THE BEAST." As he would not be an Operator, he became a Speculator, and soon learned the arts of diplomacy, politics and trade. He raised Charles II to the throne, and restored monarchy to England, and proved that his secret diplomacy was stronger than the armies of Cromwell. He shook the world with politics, wars and revolution, and when the blood of the martyrs was shed, he held the garments of them that slew them. From him the ministers of the Church received their appointments, and the legislators and judges of the State, their places. The Church dared not expel him, and the State dared not punish him, though he was both an idolator and a murderer. If any one betrayed his secrets, he swore by the gods of his mother he would kill all such. The Scriptures foretold this fact, that he should have "power to speak, and cause that as many as would not worship the Image of the Beast, should be killed." Therefore he waxed great, and controlled the commerce of the world. No man could succeed in business, whom he opposed, and none could with either profit or safety, buy or sell in the market, without the marks of the Beast, which he had the power to make. He spared the enemies of his country in war, because they were heathens and could give him the sign, to the injury of Christian patriots who could not give it. Rebold, who wrote his biography, says when he was making higher degrees, there were charges of fraud against him, "well sustained;" that he used fraudulent dates and forged history; that his violent conduct caused the death of his mother, Operative Masonry; and the Man of Sin, his father, fell out with him and tried to excommunicate and outlaw him, but he could not be killed by paper thunder nor Papal Bulls.

Add to this the fact that Protestant countries have limited, and for a time suppressed the Masonic institution, in proof that all governments were imperiled by it. Add to this another fact, that the religion of the Masonry of our day and country, is the religion of a heathen and of an anti-Christ. The "Masonic Lexicon," page 402, says: "The religion of Masonry is pure Theism, upon which its different members engraft their own peculiar opinions; but they are not permitted to introduce them into the Lodge nor connect their truth or falsehood with the truth of Masonry."

Such is the religion of Masonry, as defined by the Masonic Dictionary, which is nothing in advance of the religion of Paine; for he was also a Theist. The religion of Paine and Masonry are alike without the Law and the Prophets, the Holy Spirit and the Redeemer, Christ Jesus; yet it professes to save mankind by its teachings. O, what a strong delusion!

The religion of Masonry cannot be true unless Christianity be false. But the Christian Mason may answer, "We are permitted to engraft our faith in

Christ, and our opinions on Theism, the Masonic stock." We reply, you are not permitted to introduce Christ nor your opinions into the Lodge, nor to connect their truth or falsehood with the truth of Masonry. Your grafting cannot be done in the Lodge, for you are forbidden to connect the truth or falsehood of your faith with the truth of Masonry. We call earth to witness that by their own showing, there is no Savior Jesus Christ in a Masonic lodge. How can men love him, who, when entering, know that they leave him behind? Must not the words of Paul disquiet them? "If any man love not the Lord Jesus Christ, let him be Anathema Maranatha." Must not the Savior be grieved at, and insulted by a gospel that cannot save? Should not a man fear to preach another gospel, when it is twice said of such a preacher: "let him be accursed?"

Again, God requires of man "that at the name of Jesus, every knee should bow, and that every tongue should confess that Jesus Christ is Lord, to the glory of God the Father." But the Masonic knee will not bow, and the Masonic tongue will not confess that Jesus Christ is Lord, to the glory of God the Father. Therefore, Masonry is an anti-Christian power, opposed to the Father and the kingdom of His Son. Let not Masons boast that their religion is pure Theism; they have no living God. There is no living God but the Father of our Lord Jesus Christ, and Masons know him not; for "whosoever denies the Son, the same has not the Father." Their God is, therefore, a false god, whom the wild and guilty fancy of Masons has clothed with their distorted ideas of the Christian's God. As the religion of Christians is older than the sects to which they belong, and as ancient as the worship of Christ, so the religion of Masonry is older than Masonry, and as ancient as the worship of Bacchus, the god of Masons, whose identity has been preserved by the oath-guarded doors of his temple, and the death-guarded secrets of his worship. Masons themselves have often erred by mistaking the Masonic religion for the Masonic organization.

We now call the reader's attention to the latter, in connection with the advantages it gives to traders and thieves, clergymen and politicians, criminals and speculators, etc. There are other mysteries besides those of Bacchus in the Masonic organization. It is so mysteriously constructed out of such mystic materials, that the opposition of good men strengthens it, and when they convince mankind that they are speaking the truth about Masonry, it increases the number of those who join it. The second mystery is, why an institution said to be so good, should be by an organic and irreversible law made so limited; and why Masons have found it to their interest to hold back the increase of their own membership, and thus prevent the development of their religion. We have, therefore, an institution that is restrained by the action of its friends, and increased by the opposition of its foes. Again, it is believed by thousands of men, and Masons in particular, that they have invented a kind of oath which, when a man takes, it makes it right for him to do wrong, and wrong for him to do right. This is another mystery.

On the first mystery we remark, there are two distinct classes of men concerned in it. First, one class of right-minded men who are the salt of the earth, and will not take an unjust advantage of any man. Second, there is another class who have decided to take every advantage in their power over all others, and spend nothing for charitable purposes. Not one of this class will join the fraternity as long as they believe there is one word of truth in what Freemasons say of themselves; that their money goes for charitable purposes, and that they are self-sacrificing and pure. But as soon as an anti-Mason fully convinces them that all this is false, that the Masonic institution is selfish and uncharitable—that men join it for the unjust advantage it gives them over the rest of mankind, and the protection it affords to thieves and criminals, their minds at once become changed, and they will say within themselves, "that is just what suits me, the very thing, I will join it." So an anti-Mason generally drives ten scoundrels into it, for every good man he induces to come out of it, while moral cowards fly into it to keep from being injured by it.

It would seem that the pagan religion of Masonry might soon cover the world, the Church be shaken from her foundation and all man's hopes of heaven fail, were not Masonry bound by its own oaths and interests; were not Masons sworn that women should never worship at their altar; did they not exclude the poor, the cripple and the slave; did they not see that if it became universal there would be none left for them to wrong; and were they not sworn on pain of death that they would never reveal the mystery of their heathen worship to the outside world, and therefore cannot propagate it, save in the darkness of the Lodge. Thus Masonry is bound with its own oaths and interests. Having the religion of the Dragon, it seems as though some angel with a great chain in his hand, had laid hold of it and bound it in a Masonic prison for a thousand years, where it is now under chains of darkness. How strange that Oddfellows should boast of having three links of this chain!

In regard to the mystery of the oath which Freemasons have invented, which, when a man takes it, makes it right for him to do wrong, that he may keep it, and wrong for him to do right, lest he break it, we remark, that if Masons have invented such an oath as this they have outwitted the Almighty, and reversed the action of His moral government. If there is binding power in an oath, it derives that power from God in whose name it is taken. An oath of this kind would array one part of his government against another, divide the unity of his kingdom and bring it to naught. This Masonic mystery is a strong delusion, which, if Masons believe, they believe a lie; and unless they seek and receive mercy from Him whose government they are trying to destroy, they all must be damned. However, their oath would not be such a great evil to society at large as it is, if they were bound by it to injure none but Freemasons; but instead of this, they say: "I furthermore promise and swear that I will not wrong this Lodge, nor a brother of this degree, to the value of a cent;" and "furthermore do I promise and swear that I will not violate the chastity of a Master Mason's wife, mother, sister nor daughter, I knowing them to be such."

Now, if a Freemason is a dishonest man, he may be restrained from acts of dishonesty towards a Mason by this oath: and if lustful, from exercising his propensity upon a Freemason's nearest female relatives, should he know them to be such. Neither of his vices are cured by his oath, but only turned another way and let loose upon society. His dishonesty is so directed that others than Masons must bear it, and his lust is satisfied upon other men's wives, mothers, sisters and daughters. The whole seems to be a plan to make society bear the injury and pain resulting from Masonic sin. Thus is another mystery explained.

The Masonic oaths and penalties so often made and repeated in every degree of Masonry, each conflicting with others, and all contrary to the civil oath and the duties and vows of Christianity, and frequently clashing with the oaths, vows and pledges of other secret societies to which many Masons belong, render it impossible for men thus bound to perform the requirements of their complex obligations. Hence, many in despair or derision, wil regard no oath or obligation whatever, and the example being contagious, the foundations of society seem almost ready to dissolve.

The line of argument, which began at the tenth century, has reached the nineteenth. As everything was disputed or new, everything had to be argued or proved. So short was the space allowed, we have attempted to express in a sentence what might have filled a chapter. The object has been to first trace the history, and then state the character of modern Masonry. Both these are parts of a larger conception, a condensed view of which may be given that the leading idea be not lost in the particulars.

*First:*—Modern Masonry is the issue of the Roman Corporations of Builders, known in Masonic Rituals as Operative Masonry.

*Second:*—The germ of its existence was formed by the adulterous connection of the Catholic Church with the pagan institutions of the Roman Empire.

*Third:*—The germ was quickened by the Catholic Priesthood, and leaped with strength while it was yet in the dark womb of Operative Masonry.

*Fourth:*—It was fully endowed with life in the fourteenth century, when Pope Benedict issued diplomas which stamped its character in all subsequent generations of its existence.

*Fifth:*—In the sixteenth century it enlarged itself by the Order of Jesuits, which the Pope confirmed with a decree.

*Sixth:*—It further enlarged itself with great rapidity after this event, in 1649, by "the institution of many degrees hitherto unknown, which, in fact, gave to this time-honored institution a character entirely political." It is now that its puissant arm reverses the actions of the armies of Cromwell, "lifts Charles II to the throne, and restores monarchy to England."

*Seventh:*—It next buried Operative Masonry, its Maternal Companion, in the last sands of the seventeenth century, its wars and violence having destroyed it.

*Eighth:*—In 1717, it set up for itself entirely independent of the Builders.

As the germ and origin of Speculative Masonry are found in the Middle Ages, it is not necessary to our purpose to prove the exact date of his birth, whether it was in the womb or the arms of Operative Masonry before 1717; but having regarded Rebold as the historian of the Image, we have adopted the latter opinion.

*Ninth:*—It grew rapidly, mostly by means of the Jesuits, till the close of the eighteenth century, when Masons began to combine their Rites and lessen the number of degrees.

*Tenth:*—In its present condensed and approved form, it well-nigh controls the Church, and the politics and trade of the land.

When we compare the history and character of Masonry with that of the Image, we find them agreeing in every particular. The Image is an artificial superstructure, made in imitation of the Empire, the ten-horned Beast, in the period of Catholic domination in Europe; without any internal principle of life of its own, it artificially receives it from the Catholics, the two-horned Beast. So Masonry, not the government of the Empire, but the mere image of it is, in its origin, intimately connected with the Catholic Church, yet distinct from it; *imperium in imperio,* or rather the third government within the boundary of the first, contemporary with the second, immoral, sinful and idolatrous, is itself a living idol, enforcing its own worship with the penalty of death. We affirm without fear, that all these things, in particular and in the whole, exist nowhere else but in Masonry, and here they are all to be found in perfection. So Masonry and the Image stand looking at each other, as a man beholding himself in a glass, and they are likely to stand so till men fully comprehend the relation they bear to each other. The recognition of this fact must and will cause its death to ensue. How can Masonry live after it is perceived to be only an image belonging to the Beast, which only perishing men worship—men whose names are not written in the Book of Life, but who become heirs to every woe pronounced upon all those who worship the Beast and his Image, and who receive the mark of his name.

If there were no other arguments to be offered than those already presented, would not the testimony of concurrent circumstances and the requisite characteristics, including the proper time, place and producing causes, be sufficient to prove that our position is too strong to be false? But for the sake of those who are slow to believe, it may be added, as the Scriptures cannot be broken, therefore if Freemasonry is not the Image of the Beast, something else is. That something else must bear the same relation to the Roman Empire and the Roman Catholic Church that Freemasonry does, being made in imitation of the one and receiving life from the other; being distinct from either and existing contemporaneously with both. It must also be and do as Freemasonry is and does. An organization of this kind is very hard to find; but let the doubtful search for it in everything civil and ecclesiastical; then let them walk through vacant places seeking images and finding none, till tired of the search. They will return, we trust, to tell us they saw their failure far plainer than the Image.

# CHAPTER VII.

The proof that the ten-horned Beast is the Roman Empire may be found in another chapter. The fact has been acknowledged by Christians in the time of Constantine and by Irenæus, and also by the Church in modern times.

If the Beast is the Empire, then the image of the Beast is the image of the Empire; or, the image of the Empire is the image of the Beast; or, Freemasonry, if Freemasonry is the image of the Empire. The image of Cæsar on the tribute money, spoken of in the Gospel, could not certainly be distinguished from any other by those not informed; hence the question: "Whose image is it?" None but those acquainted with the Emperor could recognize his image on the penny. So also, some acquaintance with the Empire is necessary, in order to recognize its image in Freemasonry. The marks of the Beast are most distinctly made in the lower degrees, and the Image is most distinctly seen in the higher degrees of Masonry.

The Empire has had its image taken: Freemasons are the artists who took it, and their own institution is the picture. As the germinal formation of Masonry took place in the Middle Ages, therefore this picture must be the image of the Empire in the Middle Ages. If the image character of Masonry is complete; if there is a true representation in it, of the religions, peoples and institutions of the Middle Ages, such as to form an Image of the Empire, then shall we find something in Masonry to correspond to everything of moment in the institutions of the Empire, as well as all the moral attributes of the Beast; that is to say, we shall find the moral as well as the artificial image of the Empire in Masonry. Everything contained in the Empire must appear in the Image. The heathen mysteries, rites and religion which still lingered in the Empire, must appear there with their myths and legends. The Catholic religion, its pageantry and titles, its deacons, priests and pontiffs, must appear there. A confused and blasphemous mixture of these things might be expected in the image of such an Empire, together with its civil government, its kings and rulers. Add to this the fact that the moral sympathies and actions of the Beast must also be found in his living and speaking image.

In order to examine the subject carefully, we will divide the Empire into two general departments, the civil and religious. The religious may again be divided into Catholic and heathen. Heathenism, at the opening of the Middle Ages, was considerable, and seems to have continued to exist to their close. The Germans, and more particularly the Saxons north of the Danube, were mostly unconquered and unconverted heathens at the close of the eighth century, and Charlemagne who finally conquered and tried to convert them, according to Gibbon's history, was himself a half-converted heathen with nine wives and concubines. Gaul, Britain and Germany were countries where the Druids had long practiced their mysteries and secret rites, so closely imitated by Freemasons, and sacrificed human beings upon their altars. Gibbon informs us that "the Grecian rites existed in the eighth century, and were never completely abolished." A quotation from Psellus by Cross, says: "The mysteries of Ceres subsisted in Athens till the eighth century of the Christian era and were never totally suppressed." Masonic history affirms a direct connection between the heathen mysteries and those Architects who were patronized by the Popes in the Middle Ages; that is, with the Operative Masons. We might add, the Beast was wounded by heathens, and at that time the whole Empire swarmed with them.

The heathenish Masonic religion of our times is, therefore, the likeness of heathenism previously existing in the Empire. A religion without a Savior, that knew not Jesus, existed in the Empire before it existed in Speculative Masonry. The heathen mysteries employed in the worship of false gods, the symbolic mode of teaching by employing such things as squares and compasses as symbols, obligations of secrecy, and signs and grips, all existing in the Empire, necessitate the likeness of such things in a well-drawn image. The Masonic death-penalties, such as cutting the throat across, tearing the breast open and taking out the heart, cutting the body in two, etc., seem to be derived from the ancient mode of sacrificing animals and men, The Druids used to examine the bleeding bodies of the human victims whom they immolated in sacrifice; and in the Eleusinian and Bacchanalian mysteries, the man who violated the vow of secrecy he had taken at his initiation, was slain and sacrificed by the fraternity of the god he worshiped. This view we believe is sustained by the highest Masonic authority. We quote from Albert Mackey's "Masonic Lexicon," under the word

"PENALTY.—* * * After an animal had been selected, his throat was cut across at one single blow, so as to divide the windpipe, arteries and veins, without touching any bone. The next ceremony was to tear the breast open and pluck out the heart, and if there was the least imperfection, the body would be considered unclean. The animal was then divided into two parts and placed north and south, that the parties to the covenant might pass between them from east to west, and the carcass was then left a prey to voracious animals." He adds:

CHAPTER VII. | 105

"The allusion will not escape the attentive Mason." We think not, while he has such practical comments to reflect upon as the case of Wm. Miller in the Belfast Lodge, whose throat was cut across, his breast opened to his heart, and his body thrown out and left unburied, a victim sacred to the Masonic god. Thus there is a heathen department in Masonry to correspond with that in the Empire.

There is also something like Christianity in Masonry. It derives this characteristic mostly from the Catholic Church, another institution of the Roman Empire with which Masonry was once closely connected. The way in which the Church of Rome began to bestow its titles and imprint its likeness on Masonry, is thus described by Rebold, page 46:

"In England, as on the Continent, the Lodges became attached to the Convents, and were more or less governed by Monks, according as the leading architects were Monks or lay brethren. From this arose the condition that lodges held their meetings almost exclusively in the Convents, where, if an Abbot was proposed as Master or Warden of a lodge, they addressed him as Worshipful Brother or Worshipful Master, thus establishing a mode of address which has descended to our own day, as the usual one in speaking to or of the first officer within a lodge."

This quotation proves first, the great affinity existing between the Catholic Church and a pagan institution of the Empire; and second, that the title by which the Master of a lodge is now addressed, is a compound of pagan and Catholic origin, indicating an admixture of heathenism and Christianity in the Masonic superstructure, corresponding with the mixed character of the religion of the Empire.

The Christian department of Masonry consists in, first, the adoption of titles peculiar to the Church, such as Junior and Senior Deacons, Wardens, Chaplains, Priests and High Priests; second, the adoption of the Christian Scriptures as a Masonic symbol, thus making the Bible of equal dignity with the Masonic square and compasses, and of no more value than the sacred books of heathen nations; third, the dedication of Lodges and orders to patron saints and persons of notoriety in the Scriptures; fourth, the adoption of striking events recorded in Scripture, as the basis of Masonic history and Masonic scenes, connected with the different Rites and Degrees; fifth, the adoption of Christian ideas, often clothed in the very same language used by the Holy Spirit in His communications to man, but much oftener the ideas are perverted while the language is employed.

In this connection we may mention that in the Lodge, the true doctrine of man's immortality is taught; but not as in the Scriptures, by the resurrection of Jesus Christ from the dead, but by the resurrection of Hiram Abiff, said by Masonic authority to be the same as Bacchus. It would seem that in order to compensate for this outrage on Christianity, they have clothed Bacchus, the Masonic god, with all the glory and honor of Jesus Christ who said, "I am the resurrection and the life," and with all the majesty and attributes of the Christians' God, whom men in celebrating heathen mysteries cannot worship, but may blaspheme. The Christian obligation to love mankind, is often bound up in oaths of murderous intent, and torn fragments of Scripture, severed from their connections, lie sparkling in diminished lustre beside Masonic myths; they beautify Masonic lectures and adorn Masonic prayers. The religion of Masonry, taken as a whole, makes the institution the religious image of the Empire in its darkest days.

Speculative Masonry, growing up amid the different forms of government prevailing in the Roman Empire, very naturally imitated those forms of government and assumed the titles of their rulers, thus growing into their image by the operation of a natural law. Hence, there are Kings, Princes, Emperors, Deacons, Priests and Pontiffs in Masonry, and these were the rulers of the civil and religious departments of the Empire. Nor are Masonic rulers destitute of similar powers. In the Rite of Mizraim, Bedarride exercised a power similar to that of the Pope. Rebold, page 183, says:

"The Sovereign Grand Council of the 90th Degree of the Grand Masters Absolute, delegated to Michael

Bedarride the same powers and all their supreme rights as therein expressed, by this patent, to create, form, regulate, dissolve, whenever desirable, Lodges, Chapters, Colleges, Directories, Synods, Tribunals, Consistories, Councils and General Councils of the Order of Mizraim."

There have existed in the Roman Empire two general forms of government, Monarchical and Hierarchical. These forms united in the Pope, and were very much interwoven throughout the Empire. Of these forms the Hierarchical was in the ascendant. The Hierarchy governed the Monarchy. The Spiritual stood above the Temporal power for hundreds of years. In this condition of things, Priests, Bishops and Popes had more power than Princes, Emperors and Kings. The Mitre governed the Crown. Now as that state of things existed in the Empire, it must also appear in its image. Accordingly Masonry employs the Hierarchical and Monarchical forms of government, and they are interwoven as in the Empire. The Masonic Mitre rules the Masonic Crown. The Forms of Installations and Coronations laid down in the "Masonic Chart," for the government of the Royal Arch Degree, page 193, contains the following:

"The institutions of political society teach us to consider the King as the chief of created beings, and that the first duty of his subjects is to obey his mandates; but the institution of our Sublime Degrees, by placing the King in a situation subordinate to the High Priest, teaches us that our duty to God is paramount to all other duties, and should ever claim the priority of our obedience to a man."

This proves that the Masonic Chapter exalts its Hierarch above its Monarch, and the Spiritual despot of the Chapter assigns the same reason for doing so, that the Spiritual despots of the Empire have always given for elevating themselves above the Kings. The Masonic Mitre confers more power than the Masonic Crown. How could it be otherwise? The Spiritual rulers of the Empire—the Bishops, Priests and Popes, were superior to Princes, Kings and Emperors. Therefore, the Masonic King was predestinated to be inferior to the Masonic Priest. In the Lodge, they both lose their titles, but retain their Monarchial and Hierarchal powers; the King in the Lodge as Senior Warden, and the High Priest as Master. (See Cross' "Chart," page 190.) Here, too, the Priest is superior to the King. Their relation to each other is the same in the Lodge, Chapter and Empire.

The installation and coronation of the Masonic Monarch, are performed by the Grand High Priest, who says: "The Scarlet Robe, an emblem of imperial dignity, should remind you of the paternal concern you should ever feel for the welfare of your Chapter," and "in presenting to you the Crown, which is an emblem of royalty," etc. In other Masonic Rites there are Emperors. Here the Masonic Monarchs are presented with a Scarlet

Robe, an emblem of imperial dignity. Scarlet is the color of the Robe worn by the Monarchs of the Roman Empire; and hence is the prophetic color of the Empire. The ten-horned Beast was Scarlet-colored. Rev. xvii: 4.

Not only do the Masonic Monarchs wear the same kind of Robe worn by the Monarchs of the Empire, but they receive their Crowns in the same way. Charlemagne and Napoleon were both crowned by the Pope. The custom was common in the Middle Ages. The Mitred despot in the Empire, bestowed the Civil Crown. The Mitred despot in Masonry, bestows the Masonic Crown.

The highest officers of the Empire, though despotic, were not hereditary, but elective. The Chair of the Pope and the Throne of the Cæsars were generally filled by some form of election. Masonry also, in this respect as in others, predestinated to conform to its great archetype, makes its highest officers elective. They do not hold their authority by hereditary right, but by some form of election.

We have now examined the Heathen, Christian and Governmental departments of the Empire and of Masonry, and have found that each department in the latter, conforms to its corresponding one in its great archetype, the former; that as in water, "face answers to face," so here, department answers to department, heathenism to heathenism, Christianity to Christianity, government to government, monarch to monarch, priest to priest, and all holding the same relation to each other in Masonry that they do in the Empire; the hierarch above the monarch, and the religious above the secular power in every rite and degree of Masonry.

Reader, how could all these coincidences happen unless it were that it might be fulfilled which was spoken by the prophet, that Masonry should be called the IMAGE OF THE BEAST?

Masonry is not only the artificial image of the Empire—it is also the moral image of the Beast. The sins of the Beast, and his moral character, are so clearly delineated in the Scriptures, that there is little left to explain. Our principal object, therefore, shall be to show that the sins of Masonry and its moral character, are the same as those of the Beast.

As there is not one holy thing in the inspired delineation of the Beast, so we claim there is not one holy thing in all the moral character of Freemasonry. If there is, it will be found where Masons place it, in their mysteries. These mysteries, Masonic Rituals and histories claim to be very ancient. If that claim is false, then the religion of Masonry, with all its rites, vows and obligations, is based upon that falsehood. If it is true, then Masons receive not their mysteries from Christ nor Moses, nor by revelation from God; but from heathens who knew not God. Masonic writers claim, in particular, to have received a knowledge of the Eleusinian and Bacchanalian mysteries of the East, and a general alliance with all the heathen rites and mysteries of Europe, Asia and Egypt, and even with the sins and idolatry of King Solomon, who forsook the God of his fathers, and went after "Ashtaroth, the goddess of the Zidonians." Some Masons say he practiced the heathen mysteries with Hiram Abiff, a descendant of the Canaanites, a people accursed for these very things, and should have all been destroyed by the Israelites.

The Eleusinian and Bacchanalian mysteries prevailed in Greece, Italy and Asia Minor. They are mentioned by Herodotus, Livy and others. They existed at Eleusis and Athens, and were in full blast when Paul "stood in the midst of Mars Hill, and said, 'You men of Athens, I perceive that in all things you are too superstitious.'" He knew by inspiration what he affirmed, and made no exception of the mysteries connected with the worship of Ceres and Bacchus. The historian of the "Masonic Chart" says, page 222, that in Asia Minor, these mysteries "retained their primitive lustre." Asia Minor was one of the great fields of labor for the Apostles, and if these mysteries had possessed anything holy or valuable in them, where they "retained their primitive lustre," would not the apostle who did not "shun to declare all the counsel of God," have declared their spotless character? But what does he say of them, our best commentators being witnesses? "Have no fellowship with the unfruitful works of darkness, but rather reprove them; for it is a shame even to speak of those things that are done of them in secret." Eph. v: 11, 12.

Dr. Macknight says: "Now all these reprovable actions which are practiced in celebrating these mysteries, are made manifest as sinful, by the gospel." Benson says: "Their mysteries which, therefore, were styled mysteries not to be spoken of, none being permitted to divulge them on pain of death; hence the word 'mystery' has its name, say grammarians, from 'to stop the mouth.' The Eleusinian mysteries were performed in the night, agreeably to the deeds of darkness committed in them. So were the Bacchanalia, and they were both full of detestable iniquity." Dr. Clarke says: "Probably alluding to the mysteries among the heathens, and the different lustrations and rites through which the initiated went, in caves and dark recesses, where these mysteries were celebrated; all which he denominates 'works of darkness,' because they were destitute of true wisdom; and 'unfruitful works,' because they were of no use to mankind, the initiated being obliged on pain of death, to keep secret what they had seen, heard and done. Hence, they were called 'unspeakable mysteries.' *Reprove them*—For their vices which are flagrant, while pretending to superior illumination. *For it is a shame even to speak,* etc.—This, no doubt, refers to the Eleusinian and Bacchanalian mysteries, which were performed in night and darkness, and were known to be so impure and abominable, especially the latter, that the Roman Senates banished them both from Rome and Italy. How the discovery of these depths of Satan was made, and the whole proceedings in the case, may be seen in Livy."

The fraternity that worshiped Bacchus, received some mark of their god, generally in their forehead or their right hand. They used secrecy and death-penalties.

If those fraternities, which Freemasonry so closely imitates were right, then Christianity is wrong; for it differs materially from them. But if Christianity is right, then those fraternities were wrong, for they are condemned by it; and so is every society which celebrates their mysteries.

But let it be remembered that all these rites and mysteries taken together, do not make Speculative Masonry. They appertain exclusively to the religion of Masonry. They are all sinful in themselves; but become exceedingly sinful in modern Masonry, where they are so allied to Christianity as to be confounded with it in a mass; where the Bible is reduced to a Masonic symbol, and where there is no more saving strength in the Lord's Sermon on the Mount, than in a sermon drawn from the Masonic Gavel; where Masons, while preserving the identity of Bacchus in the celebration of his mysteries, have clad their deified hero in all the attributes of God, and in their mysterious word "Jova," combine the title of the unoriginated Jehovah with that of earth-born Jove.

Modern Masonry much worse than trifles with the name of the self-existing *I am* and His burning symbol in the bush; it worse than trifles with the names of saints, their spotless robes, and the blood in which they are washed; and with all the sacred things of the Church and Heaven. So that like the Beast, Masonry rises up to view with blasphemy on its head, and like him, opens his mouth "in blasphemies against God, to blaspheme his name and his tabernacle, and them that dwell in heaven." Nor is this all; but enough is said to prove that Masonry presents the highest degree of spiritual wickedness ever attained by man. Neither is this all; for everything connected with the moral character of the Beast, which men either feared or loved, is found in Freemasonry, whether it be despot or despotism, secret or secretism, invulnerability, extent, power; ability to promote, defend or destroy. So that every principle which men worshiped in the Beast, is also worshiped in Freemasonry. The Beast and his Image are worshiped in connection, as shown in the Word of God.

The Masonic Organization contains the hierarchical, monarchial and despotic governmental forms of the Empire, with the dark impenetrable secrecy of the heathen rites, the binding power of the Eleusinian oaths and death-penalties, and the Bacchanalian mode of marking. In it may be found all the powers which inhere in secret government; power to surprise, to deceive, to strike without warning to the stricken, and every facility for corruption, intimidation and revenge. Freemasonry is a secret government whose legislature is always in session, whose members are all spies, whose designs are inscrutable, and whose subjects never tell their business to any man outside of the fraternity. If they do, they wither before the anger of an irresistible power, or fall by a hand unseen, which "avenges the treason" to their government "by the death of the traitor."

To administer their own government and inflict its penalties, is but the assertion of their ancient privileges conferred upon them by the bulls and diplomas of the Popes, when the "Man of Sin" infused such a vicious principle of life into the Masonic organization, as made it "both speak, and cause that as many as would not worship it, should be killed." This sanguinary regulation of Masonry, enables it to pursue in silence and safety its daring purpose; to pilfer the wealth of nations while it holds the civil power in chains.

The same reasons which united to make deluded mortals worship the Beast, now combine to make perishing men pay homage to Freemasonry. The secret Colossus, potent as its original to inspire sentiments of respect and reverence, strikes the minds of men with the same astonishment and fear which unnerved the worshiping multitudes who cried out: "Who is like unto the Beast? who is able to make war with him?"

In order to show more clearly that men worship Masonry for the same reasons that induced them to worship the Beast, we may enquire what was the character of that worship, and what were the reasons that prompted to it.

It is believed by some commentators, with great propriety, that this worship was mostly of a civil character; for the Beast was a civil power; therefore, very often, the homage rendered was from political motives. And as "all the world wondered after the Beast, whose deadly wound was healed," they worshiped him also for his tenacity of life which made him venerable with age; but probably more through fear, for he "made war with the saints and overcame them." Here then, are four reasons why men worshiped the Beast. First, because he had all the offices of the government to bestow; second, because he had recovered from his deadly wound; third, because he was old and venerable; and fourth, because he murdered his own subjects, the saints who would not worship him.

The Beast was truly venerable with age and strong in recuperative power, whether we consider him as seen by Daniel, when he first crouched beside the Tiber and successfully contended with the Latin States, the Greeks and the Carthagenians; or when as seen by John, as he arose in the fullness of his divided strength, with crowns of gold on all his horns, his imperial head vigorous and its deadly wound entirely healed, and to whom the

Dragon surrendered his "power, seat and great authority." The extreme age of the Beast was real. The extreme age of Speculative Masonry, his Image, is fictitious, or only apparent. Neither Mackey nor Rebold claims any great age for Speculative Masonry. They both trace its origin back to the Companies of Builders which existed in the Roman Empire till the close of the sixteenth century. When any Masonic writers lay any kind of claim to a more remote origin, they either cite us to some idolatrous sect of the ancients, from whom Masonry has obtained its religion; or to some company of stone masons working at their trade, from which it derives its name and symbols. But as the religion of Speculative Masonry, and the trade of Operative Masonry, or the name of that trade, do not make the organization in question, therefore Speculative Freemasonry is of comparatively modern origin.

To show that the extreme age of Speculative Masonry is only apparent, and not real, we will re-quote from Rebold's "Preface." He says of Clavel: "It is true, he mentions the Colleges of Roman Architects; but always pre-occupied in common with his predecessors, in seeking a remoter origin for Freemasonry in the Mysteries of the East, he fails to perceive that it was precisely within these Colleges that the birth of Freemasonry took place. The authors who pretend, and their number is very great, that Masonry originated at the construction of Solomon's Temple, are led into this error by the numerous allusions to that construction, which

CHAPTER VII. | 119

have place in the lectures of our Lodges of today." Here it is affirmed that the numerous allusions in Masonry to the construction of Solomon's Temple, have led Masons themselves into a great error in regard to the age and origin of Masonry. It is one of the clearest and most striking characteristics of Masonry, that the Lectures, Rituals and Obligations are so worded, and its organization so framed, as to make it appear very ancient. The Chapter and Lodge of Perfection, proceed in "due and ancient form," like all the rest; though Masonic history declares them to be creations of the eighteenth century.

Masonry could not be a true image of the Beast without appearing much older than it is. Two things are here required: it must be really younger than the Beast, and appear to be as old as the Beast; for such is the wonderful nature of the image which God has chosen to symbolize Freemasonry. For instance: if an artist had just finished making the image of an old man, and we should examine it, we would find it had as many feet and hands as the old man it represented; and that his form and features were now the inherent properties of his image. But there is no law by which his age can be transmitted to his image. It really has feet and hands, and the form and features of an old man, yet is not itself old. If the artist should point to its meagre form, its wrinkles and gray hairs, and say, "This image is very old," we should reply: The age does not inhere in this image, but in the man it represents. We know that the nature of an image is to speak falsely about its own age. It does not possess gray hairs and other signs of age, because it is old; but because it is the image of an old man. Likewise Freemasonry being an image, the great age of which it boasts, does not inhere in itself, but in the Roman Empire which it represents. It has all the marks of great age, not because it is itself so old, but because it is the image of an old Beast. It is, therefore, predestinated forever to speak falsely about its own age. It is a speaking Image, and men who do not know it, worship it on account of its fictitious age.

Although Freemasonry does not possess an equal age, it has given full proof that it does possess an equal power with the Beast, his recuperative strength and tenacity of life. The power of the Beast consisted in the civil power of the Empire and the spiritual authority of the Popes. Masonic historians relate the fact with pride, that Masonry has been legislated against and proscribed by the civil powers of the Empire, without avail; that almost every country in Europe has tried to suppress it, without success; and that Popes issued their bulls against it for the same purpose, but never could destroy it. Hence, Masonry has proved itself equal to the combined civil and spiritual powers of the Empire, and as often controlled the civil power as the civil power controlled it. The same is true of the Church. Rebold says that the Jesuits who destroyed it in one form, used it in another; and the historian of the "Chart," says, that when Freemasons found the Popes opposed to them, they changed their name to "Mopses" and went on. Thus the Beast found Freemasonry, in its Protean changes and secret movements, to be something almost as intangible as his own shadow, which pursued when he retreated, and fled when he pursued. It is true that some Freemasons were persecuted and slain, mostly by the Jesuits; but this was Mason killing Mason. But it has always appeared that Masons could kill the officers of the government as often as the officers could kill the Masons. It is very seldom that government is strong enough to take the life of a Freemason, even for the highest crime. Our own government was not strong enough to bring the murderers of Morgan to justice, even when assisted by Vigilance Committees and indignant and excited thousands, in a protracted struggle. Masonry delivered the murderers and maintained its own laws. In its nature, therefore, it cannot be restrained by any government, for it is a revolt from all governments of heaven and earth. It cannot owe allegiance to any government; therefore, logically, no Church obligation nor civil oath can be binding on a Freemason. A Masonic Lodge being an organized revolt, God never legislated for it; therefore it has not the least trace of the character of God upon it, and nothing to limit its freedom to do wrong. Its measureless strength results from its release from every obligation, human and Divine. Being outside the pale of all law, it governs itself with freedom, and gives direction to its own invincible wickedness. Masonry, like the Beast, is worshiped for its power and invincibility.

But men worshiped the Beast, not only because he was "great and terrible, and strong exceedingly," but also because he had great tenacity of life, and could and did recover from his deadly wound. From the time the Goths, who fled from the shout of the Huns, crossed the Danube, the Beast profusely bled from the stroke of the northern sword, till he seemed to all, to have yielded up his power and his life. But when he recovered, they worshiped the Beast whose deadly wound was healed.

Masonry even in its history, to some extent, fated to resemble the Beast, has also received a deadly wound, and has shown the same tenacity of life as the Beast. It was the exposure of Masonry by its own members, that gave the deadly wound, and multitudes of seceding Masons testifying to the same things. The murder of Morgan by Freemasons, and the protection of his murderers by the Fraternity, gave overwhelming proof that the exposition was true. The revelation of Morgan was soon followed by those of Bernard, Allyn and others, till Masonic signs, grips, oaths and death-penalties, with all the inside structure of the institution, were exposed to the view of all who wished to examine them. The institution, detected in falsehood, convicted of murder, defeated at the polls, pursued by the law, and scorned by the multitude, gave signs of fear that all was lost. "About two thousand Lodges were suspended," and "out of a little more than fifty thousand Masons, forty-five thousand turned their backs upon the Lodge to enter it no more." Masonry, like the Beast, received a deadly wound, from which many thought it never could recover. Certainly it ought to have died for shame, here and in every civilized country in the world. But no—it clung to life with wonderful tenacity, like its archetype, the Beast, and like him, began to recover from its wound; though it could only meet argument with silence, open rebuke with private injury, the revelation of Masonry with the Masonic laugh, and betrayal with murder. Yet with such instrumentalities, it recovered, and all the world wondered after the Artificial Beast whose deadly wound was healed.

Men worshiped the Beast because he was old, strong and tenacious of life; but much more because he was a civil power, and had all the civil offices to bestow. There was much in him they feared, and they had much to hope from him. His smile gave wealth and safety; his frown gave poverty and danger. He made men Esquires, Constables and Aldermen. He appointed Captains, Generals and other officers of the Army; placed Judges on the Bench, and raised men to the highest councils of the nation. Therefore, men worshiped the Beast for the same reasons they now worship Freemasonry; for Freemasonry is such an express image of the Beast, that it possesses a similar appointing power, and exercises it in every country where the institution is established. Rebold, the greatest of Masonic historians says, that Charles II, "in consequence of the benefits he received from the Society, gave to Masonry the title of 'Royal Art;' because it was mainly by its instrumentality that he was raised to the throne, and monarchy restored to England." Thus Masonry has power to bestow the highest offices of the civil government, and Masons seize upon lucrative positions and places of power quite out of proportion to their number or merit, and far more than they could obtain either by chance or justice. Therefore, every man of small virtue and great covetousness, will worship Masonry. How many soldiers, returning from our late war, have declared they would never go to war again without first becoming Freemasons; because they have observed that in the army, Masons have more than an honest chance of promotion, and less than an honorable chance of suffering; being in league with Masonic rebels. Therefore, all the army, except those who love equality and justice more than promotion and safety, falls down and worships Masonry.

Freemasons stand a far better chance than other men to be elevated to positions, State and National, where the laws of our country are made; and if they violate these laws, they stand a far less chance of suffering the penalties attached to them; for Masonic law defends them against the penal action of civil law, even if they should be guilty of embezzlement, treason and murder. Therefore, corrupt politicians, thieves, robbers and murderers fall down, and with their whole heart, worship Masonry.

The power Freemasonry exercises in ecclesiastical affairs, is also very great. It is a serious question, whether it does not, by means not always concealed, station or install more ministers than the Church, and whether it does not control the Church property and finances more than the membership. And it does seem that through its presence among Christians, Church trials are often conducted more in accordance with Masonic law, than with the Word of God or the Discipline of the Church. The press and the pulpit are together struck dumb in its presence, they being restrained by interest or fear, or chained to silence by the Masonic obligations taken by editors and preachers. They have not been slow to see that there is no reasonable chance of being sustained or promoted without Masonic assistance. Even those not under sworn allegiance to the Fraternity, seem to be manacled by its power, and find it impossible to oppose it without the loss of character and business. For these reasons editors and ministers, on all sides, are falling down and worshiping this Image of the Beast.

Freemasonry likewise lays its rapacious hand on trade, and covers its property with its symbols and its merchandise with marks, that Masons may secure for it the highest and quickest sales in the market, and to protect it from Masonic rapine; for Masonic thieves are sworn on the peril of their lives, not to touch it to the injury of a Mason. Thus it seems to give some dishonorable advantage in every department of society, so that none but the upright will refuse to pay it homage.

Masonry is the Image of that Beast, of whom it was said: "All that dwell upon the earth shall worship him, whose names are not written in the book of life." But God has reserved to himself more than seventy times seven thousand, who have not bowed the knee to the Image of the Beast.

In order to explain the whole subject fully, we must advert once more to the fact that Freemasonry is the image of the Roman Empire during the Middle Ages, and that it ought to and does contain the likeness of both its Church and Civil Government. The reasons which prove this, are clear and strong.

*First:*—The Church was an Empire within an Empire; that is, the Civil Empire contained the Church; hence, its true image should contain the same things in representation, that are contained in the Empire.

*Second:*—Church Government became Civil Government, whenever it exercised the powers of Civil

Government. Whenever ecclesiastical law became the civil law of the Empire, then it was both civil and ecclesiastical law. This kind of government continued in full force from Charlemagne to Charles V., about seven hundred years, and should and does exist in Freemasonry, the perfect image of the Empire.

We have elsewhere shown that Masonry contains the image of the civil power of Rome, its kings and rulers. We here add, it takes upon itself the airs of a civil power, and seems to think it really is one. It has a Legislature and Judiciary, which exercise the highest functions of civil government. It tries, condemns, and it executes its subjects, on whom it has passed the sentence of death.

Masonry is also the speaking Image of the Church of Rome, whose behests were incorporated into the laws of the State, and whose mandates became the dominant governmental power, in all the ten kingdoms of the Beast. Masonry assumes its titles and asserts its powers; for the secret nominees of the institution are the rulers of Church and State. Like the Catholic Church, it governs governments; it usurps their rights, performs their functions, and directs their powers; and is so much like a dominant universal Church, that it seems to think it really is one. It has a universal religion and liturgy, deacons, priests and other Church officers. It performs the office of a Church, when it undertakes to show to mankind the way of salvation, and to promise eternal life to all who obey it. Thus it steals and plunders away the inherent rights of Church and State, and is the image of them both.

Masonry also contains a complete image of the Roman Corporations of Builders and the mysteries which they practiced. It is said that these Corporations originated in the infancy of Rome, when the successor of Romulus divided the tradesmen into different societies, and applied some provision of the twelve tables of Roman law, to each society. These trades-unions, which worshiped a man-made god, originated at the foundation of Roman society. Their origin is thus described by Rebold, page 378: "The mysteries of Eleusis were imported by Roman initiates, from Greece. This worship, adopted by the great legislator, Numa Pompilius, became the basis of the religious ceremonies and the initiations of the Colleges of the Builders founded by him." Their existence has been traced by Masons, down through the Middle Ages. Their mysteries are noticed by Pliny, who lived when Jesus began preaching in Galilee. These Corporations and mysteries were of the Empire, the Beast, and Freemasonry contains their image. Here we defy contradiction.

These Colleges "were both civil and religious institutions." They were one of the primary divisions of the Empire. They were stone-masons and builders. They had master builders, master masons and craftsmen, and they received apprentices who wished to learn the trade. But no apprentice was received by them, till he had first gone through the initiatory ceremonies of the mysteries of Bacchus and Ceres, whom they worshiped. The apprentices had to swear under the penalty of death, to conceal the art of building and the religious mysteries from the rest of mankind. By concealing the art of building, they monopolized the trade and raised their wages. When working on a large superstructure, they made a temporary building for themselves, called a Lodge. In order that no others should obtain a knowledge of their art, and they lose their monopoly, they were taught grips and signs of recognition; and none but able-bodied men, who could build were admitted into the fraternity.

To show the image character of the modern Lodge, we may compare it with the former College. The College had much that was literal and real; the Lodge is filled with imagery, symbolism and representation. The former was a legal establishment in the civil compact, which existed from the infancy of Rome to the close of the seventeenth century, and was, in the language of Rebold, "both a civil and religious institution." It was religious, because it really worshiped Bacchus and practiced his mysteries, administered the oaths and enforced the death-penalties of his worship, in connection with those of Eleusis and other heathen rites. The members were called Masons, because they worked at the trade of Masonry, and taught their apprentices how to hew rocks and build houses out of them.

A working Lodge of Master Masons is a representation of a College of Builders. It is not a College, but a representation of one. It assumes the name Mason, without working at the trade. It has Master Masons to teach; Fellows of the Craft to labor; and receives Apprentices, swears them with the same old Bacchanalian oaths, and threatens them with the same penalties. It then puts the same working tools into their hands, and sets them to work on some imaginary building; when the whole confraternity go to work, spreading cement with trowels, circumscribing with the compasses, dividing with the gauge and pounding with the mallets of the Builders.

That the College was an institution of the Beast, and that the Lodge is its image, are truths supported by that kind of evidence which compels belief. As an idol represents a god, so does a Master's Lodge represent a College of Builders. The histories, rituals and revelations teem with the evidence of this fact.

As a Lodge of Master Masons represents the Builders of the Empire, so do the Knights Templars represent its military power. Their swords and titles, their Commanderies, Encampments and military tactics, prove to reflecting minds, that they represent the Crusades, the Armies of the Beast.

If we had been merely able to discover in Masonry the image of the Civil Government of the Empire, we might then have claimed that we had proved that Masonry is the Image of the Beast. But when we have shown that it also contains the image of the Church, the evidence is doubled. When it is made clear that it contains the image of the Builders of the Empire, the evidence is tripled; and as it contains the image of the Armies of the Empire, the evidence is quadrupled. Finally, when it is ascertained that when the moral qualities of Masonry are added to the foregoing facts, they together not only correspond harmoniously with their originals in the Empire, but completely form an image of the Beast, the evidence becomes overwhelming. We may add, in this connection, that Masons have held something like the same views; that is, that the imagery and skill of Operative Masons made their superstructures capable "of faithfully reflecting the *Image* and sentiments indicative of the then civil and religious knowledge of the peoples."—Rebold, page 76. The reflection of the civil and religious knowledge and sentiments of the Roman people, or an image indicative of them, was an image of the Empire.

A condensed view of the ideas contained in this chapter, may be stated thus: Freemasonry is a kind of theatrical representation and pictorial imagery of the Roman Empire of the Middle Ages; that is, the different Rites and degrees of Masonry contain a representation or living picture of the religions, peoples, builders, armies, emperors, kings, princes, priests, prelates, popes, governments, principles and other characteristics of the Roman Empire, the Beast. It seems more fitting to dare the reader to deny, than to entreat him to believe this; since the facts are stubborn, and truth, when understood, compels belief. Therefore, Freemasonry is a vast Image Empire, co-existing and co-extensive with the Beast.

# CHAPTER VIII.

In order to show more forcibly that Freemasonry is as nearly related and as closely connected to the Roman Empire and the Catholic Church, as the Image is to the first and second Beasts, we will divide the institution into two elements or classes: first, that which was something else before it was Masonry, and was afterwards transformed into the Order of today; and second, that which was never anything else but Masonry, and therefore having nothing of a material or tangible nature entering into its composition. By the former division, Masonry is connected with the Empire, and by the latter, with the Church.

In the case of the first species of Masonry, we behold, in history, the successive descent into Secretism, of certain civil and other orders of the Roman Empire—a kind of retirement into a secret or invisible continuation. Between these orders thus withdrawn from civil and open existence, and certain Masonic Rites for high degrees, as well as the English Rite of three degrees, a strong bond of union was established, which resulted in a considerable change in the original nature of the orders. They have been so transformed by Masonic manipulation and re-handling, that they now look more like parodies on the original orders of the Empire, than retired continuations of them. Nevertheless they constitute the most important and substantial part of modern Masonry. The change by which these orders were assimilated to the Masonic system and became incorporated into its being, passed upon them in the early part of the eighteenth century. Their decline into secrecy took place in different cases, from fifty to four hundred years before that time, and even more than that. In other instances, originating in something else, they were immediately changed into Masonry, as in the case of the Illuminati.

The second kind of Masonry, which was never anything else but Masonry, consists in imitations of the civil orders of the Empire. The Empire contained many models for this kind of Masonic mimicry. There are many Masonic orders of Knighthood; yet there is but one, at most two, of such orders that can be traced back to their points of juncture with civil Knighthood, which was the equestrian order of nobility in the middle ages.

The first kind of Masonry arose from certain declining and dying orders of the Roman Empire, which, seeing their end approaching, made a descent into Secretism to save from extinction a name and remnant which could not otherwise be preserved. The Colleges of Builders

CHAPTER VIII. | 135

and chartered stone-masons are among this number. Thus something like Freemasonry first began to be produced. A vain struggle was maintained for many years by these orders to regain their former positions. Failing in this, the unclean and troubled spirits of these perishing institutions walked through dry places, seeking rest and finding none, till at last, as if by common consent, in the eighteenth century, they united to form a secret, invisible empire of their own, from whence, with thievish hands, they might rob the social compact, and stay the justice of the civil arm. From this foul and secret confederation has developed that angry but concealed struggle of Masonry with civil government, which has been continued ever since the formation of the mystic and mischievous union. The proof of this will be given hereafter.

The Jesuits were the real fathers of the second species of Masonry, though it was imitated by infidels and others. The following are the circumstances which gave birth to this element of the Masonic system:

Certain members of the Church of Scotland, and degenerate children of Bruce, who first occupied the throne of Scotland, and after the death of Elizabeth, the throne of England, while professing the Protestant religion, continually gravitated toward Catholicism and absolutism. In the struggle which ensued, Charles I, was beheaded. Charles II, after professing the religion of Scotland at Scone, where he was crowned, was defeated by Cromwell and driven to France. There, as Robinson and Rebold tell us, he was made a Freemason, and by that means re-established monarchy and became king of England. The historian informs us that "by receiving in his last moments the sacrament from a Popish priest, proved that he lived a hypocrite as well as a libertine." His successor, James II., "suspended the exercise of the Protestant religion, acknowledged the supremacy of the Pope, and allowed the Jesuits to establish themselves in the kingdom." From henceforward the royal family of the house of Stuart seem to have been both Roman Catholics and Freemasons. One of them was a Cardinal and died in Rome. The royal family and their partisans figure very largely in Masonic history.

The Baron Ramsay, whom Fenelon made a Catholic, spread the new Jesuit Masonry in France and England. Charles Edward Stuart, born at Rome, son to the first Pretender, founded a chapter of high degrees at Arras.

But to return to the times of Charles and James. Prof. Robinson informs us that "at this time the Jesuits interfered considerably, insinuating themselves into the Lodges." "And we know that at this time they were by no means without hope of re-establishing the dominion of the Church of Rome in England; and their services were not scrupled at by the distressed Royalists."—*Proofs of a Conspiracy*, page 21.

Nor did this hope seem unreasonable. The house of Stuart was allied to the throne of France by marriage, to the chair of St. Peter by religion, and to Masonry by the mystic tie. Scotland and Ireland were ready to take up arms. The Jesuits, as Macaulay says, having turned the tide of battle in favor of Catholicism, Protestantism, which, during that whole generation, had carried all before it, was stopped in its progress by them and rapidly beaten back from the foot of the Alps to the shores of the Baltic. Surely those Jesuits thought by combining all these forces they could re-establish the Catholic religion in England.

The Jesuits were a grade of Catholics, who, nearly two hundred years before the above period, had gone down into secret existence, and had become quite skilled in secret politics. They now went to work with a will, inventing new political kinds of Masonry, and changing the old, to be propagated and worked by the royal family and all their partisans in Rome, France and England.

It was, therefore, the great contest for Catholic ascendancy that gave rise to the second branch of Masonic constituency, which, not originating in anything else, needed not to be, to use Masonic language, "resuscitated under Masonic forms," like the first department.

The first division connects Masonry with the Roman Empire; the second unites it with the Church of Rome. These two, originally distinct features of the Masonic order, have been so fused together by the hands of the Jesuits, that neither three-degree Masons nor Masonic councils have ever been able to separate them. In vain does Rebold complain, page 217, "how completely the object desired by the Jesuits was effected. 'Confusion worse confounded' reigned among the Fraternity; false titles antedated constitutions; charges of fraud well sustained, and even exhibitions of violence characterized the Masonic institution, and the civil government had to interfere to prevent worse results."

It is true that Barruel, himself a Catholic, labors feebly to relieve the Jesuits from the blame cast upon them by Robinson for using Masonry in English politics; but the fact is not only stated and re-stated, but everywhere crops out in Rebold's History of Masonry. And the internal evidence of those higher degrees called Christian, will sustain these authorities on this point.

We will now call the reader's attention more particularly to that division of Masonry which connects the institution with the civil and other orders of the Roman Empire, and which, having been something else before it was Masonry, needed to be changed or "resuscitated under Masonic forms."

In order to show the nature of Masonic formations of this class, we will notice something of the kind that has transpired in our country.

Polygamy and Polytheism are errors inherent in Mormonism. Joseph Smith was not a Freemason when he professed the discovery of the Plates and brought out the book of Mormon; yet the great body of Mormons in Utah have burrowed into the dark realm of Secrecy, and adopted Masonic forms. The Mormon endowment is little more than Masonic initiation, for it has the penalties of the first three degrees of Masonry attached to it, and has the appearance of a new Masonic Rite. They even swear to avenge the death of Joseph Smith, as the Templars swear to avenge the death of their Grand Master, Molay. See Beadle's "Life in Utah."

The temperance reformation which started in our country in the days of the Washingtonians, furnishes another illustration. Sometime after it arose it divided, and one part dropped down into Secretism and fell far below the plain when the other remained. This descent resulted in two formations, both of which became united to the Masonic family, by adopting Masonic forms, under which to operate, though they were not assimilated into the Masonic institution proper. These new secret corporations were the Sons of Temperance and Good Templars. In the latter we find an oath and the very name of the Masonic Knight, "Templar." Other orders of a similar nature, for various purposes, have since been in like manner created.

In the list of names of Masonic Rites, given by Rebold, we find the Rite of Swedenborg. Barruel informs in regard to the origin of this Rite. He says that from among the disciples of Swedenborg "arose two distinct sects; the one public, the other occult." *Memoirs*, Vol. IV, page 138.

The religion of Swedenborg was not orthodox. We shall not stop to decide whether it was Christianity or only refined materialism; or whether his visions were real, or only the dreamy madness of a disordered brain. But we wish to state the fact that a part of his followers separated from the rest, and formed a Masonic Rite, making a descent into Secretism almost to the verge of hell, and taking refuge, according to Barruel, "in the dens of Rosicrucian Masonry." Taking the name of Theosophical Illuminees, they became assimilated to the name and character of the Illuminati of Weishaupt. Their oath is as follows:

"I here break all the ties of flesh that bind me to father, mother, brothers, sisters, wife, relations, friends, mistresses, kings, chiefs, benefactors; in short, to every person to whom I have promised faith, obedience, gratitude or service. I swear to reveal to the new chief, whom I acknowledge, everything that I shall have seen, done, read, learned or discovered; and even to seek after and spy into things that might otherwise escape my notice. I swear to revere the *Aqua Topana* as a certain, prompt and necessary means of ridding the earth, by death or stupefaction, of those who revile the truth, or seek to wrest it from my hands."

"Scarcely has the candidate pronounced this oath, when the same voice (the chief) informs him that from that instant he is released from all other oaths, oaths that he has taken either to his country or to the laws." *Memoirs*, Vol. IV, page 357.

Barruel adds. "Thus did this atrocious sect form its adepts, springing from the delirious reveries of Swedenborg."

The *Aqua Topana* is "a fluid containing arsenic, and used for secret poisoning, made by a woman named Topana, who is said to have poisoned six hundred persons."—*Webster*.

It would seem that a surrender as complete as this, if made to Christ, would secure the new birth. This oath, therefore, must surely obtain a birth into the kingdom of death and hell. Such an oath, taken by a Christian, crucifies the Son of God afresh, and is like the unpardonable sin.

## ROSICRUCIANS.

We find among the Masonic Rites given by Rebold, the "Rite of the Rose Cross;" and in Bernard, the degree of Rose Croix Masonry, with the Rose and Cross on the jewel and compasses of the Rose Croix Masons.

This Rite was not always Masonry, but existed in the Empire in another form before it was incorporated into the Masonic order. It was worked by the Alchemists who were known as Brothers of the Rose Cross, or Rosicrucians. Their "Cross represented the sanctity of union, and the Rose was the image of discretion." The great propagator of the Rosicrucian association, was an Alchemist, whose name was "Christian Rose Croix" and its founder's name was "Valentine Andrea." "This society was resuscitated under Masonic forms, in Germany, in 1767." See Rebold's Preface.

The Rose Croix Masons take their name from Rose Croix, and the name and emblems of the Rosicrucians. This origin is more than once stated by Rebold, and must bear down the partial denial, the faint acknowledgement, and the acknowledged ignorance of Mackey upon this subject, who seems to have been ashamed and terrified at the account, in Barruel and Robinson, about Rosicrucianism and Rosicrucian Masonry, and felt that he could not recognize such wretched ancestry; although Barruel testified what he knew, that the Scotch Knighthood of France was Rosicrucian, "Rose Crucis, or Rosicruciaus."

Their theology proves that they were not orthodox, nor decent heretics. Their "Jahova" was at once the god of good and the god of evil, and they had a number of good and evil genii, all of which know the past, present and future. "The Cabalistic Rosicrucian Mason sees apparitions of these genii. They will appear to him, and will explain more to him in the magic table, than the human understanding can conceive. From whencesoever these genii or devils may come, it is from them alone that the adept can learn the occult sciences, which infuse into him the spirit of prophecy. He will be informed that Moses, the prophets and the three kings had no other teachers and no other art but that of Cabalistic Masonry." *Memoirs,* Vol. II, page 327.

They taught magic, exorcism, witchcraft, fortune-telling, transmutation of metals, universal medicine, and Robinson adds, astrology, ghost raising and Masonry. These things demonstrate that the Rosicrucian Alchemists professed the black art, fused with Masonry, and formed a Masonic Rite. Rebold tells us the juncture took place in Germany, in 1767. Moreover it appears that these Cabalistic Masons were the true successors of "Jannes and Jambres, who withstood Moses," and by familiar spirits and magic wrought opposing miracles to those of Moses, which latter were sanctions to the command, "Let my people go."

The conflict with Moses, which was begun by the magicians of Egypt, has been continued by the Rosicrucians Masons of the eighteenth century, who declare that Moses and the prophets had no other teacher and no other art but that of Cabalistic Masonry.

These men of lying wonders still degrade the miracles of Moses to a level with their own, and antagonize by opposing miracles, everything that is or seems like, supernatural power. If others affirmed that the prayer of faith had saved the sick and raised him up, they asserted that they had done the same with their universal medicine. And if the contemporaneous priest declared that in the Mass the bread was changed by miracle into flesh, and the wine to blood, the transmutation of lead to gold by magic touch, would prove that they could do the same with their enchantments.

It is strange that modern Masons should take so much pains as they do to prove and maintain a connection between the magicians and mysteries of Egypt and their own. Their reliance on secrecy, their principles and lying wonders are the same; and the apostle Paul more than appears to recognize that identity which Masons seek so anxiously to establish. The apostle foretells the failure of the faith and search of modern reprobates in almost the same language that Mackey uses to describe the failure of the search of modern Masons after a knowledge of God, "ever learning and never able to come to the knowledge of the truth." "Now as Jannes and Jambres withstood Moses, so do these also resist the truth." Thus the apostle, with one inspired sentence, arches the gulf of ages, and connects and identifies the religion and mysteries of Masonry with the magicians and sorceries of Egypt, thereby accomplishing in a moment of time as much as Masonic writers have done in the labors of a hundred years.

Though Barruel, Robinson and Rebold found Rosicrucianism taught as high degrees of Masonry, yet it originated in a wild search for gold. When chemistry was in its infancy and had not yet settled the question whether gold was a primary element or a compound substance like brass, the idea presented itself to the Alchemists that the precious metal might be obtained in great abundance from cheap material; and if the art could be kept secret, it would secure immense fortunes for themselves and their children. This covetous instinct caused a retirement of the Alchemists into Secretism, where many of them sunk their fortunes in the crucible. The most extravagant writings by Valentine Andrea, a Catholic Monk, gave expression and form to the gold mania. They now professed to have discovered a universal medicine, and the philosopher's stone that turned everything into gold.

Such is the origin of the society of the Rose Cross, or Rosicrucians, which Rebold tells us was founded by Valentine Andrea, in 1616, and resuscitated under Masonic forms in 1767; or in much plainer words, when it could no longer be concealed that their philosopher's stone was only initiation fees and counterfeit coin, and their universal medicine no better than Dutch beer and rye whiskey, they abandoned chemistry, and to save themselves from extinction, fled into Masonry, the common receptacle of all the defunct orders of the Roman Empire.

## THE JEWS.

The migration of the Jews into Europe is a matter of history. It is well known that they believe in the Jehovah of the Old Testament, but not in Jesus Christ of the New. They say that to admit the claims of Christ to divinity, would be destructive of the unity of God. They say he has taken the name of God, which expresses unity, while his claims destroy it.

Rebold informs us that a part of Masonry is of Jewish origin. Barruel asserts that the legend of the last name in Masonic mysteries, which Masons are required to search for, is taken from the Chaldaic pharaphrase, and is "a fable invented by the Rabbins to rob Christ of his divinity and power. They supposed that Christ, being one day in the Temple of Jerusalem, had seen the Holy of Holies, where the High Priest alone had a right to enter; that he there saw the name of Jehovah; that he carried it away with him; and that by virtue of this ineffable name he had wrought his miracles."

Thus the tenets of the Jews are maintained, while an onslaught is made on those of Christianity by Jewish Masonry.

CHAPTER VIII. | 147

# THE ROYAL ARCH.

Masonic formations are governed by a common law. That law which has governed the formation of the first three degrees, has governed the formation of many. It would be useless to deny, and scarcely necessary to prove, that the descent of stone-masons into secret existence, was the proximate cause which gave birth to the first three degrees of Speculative Masonry, where their name and working-tools are still retained. Causes analogous to this have governed the formation of other degrees, Swedenborgian Masonry was created by the descent into hidden existence of Swedenborgians. Rosicrucian Masonry came into being by the withdrawal of the Alchemists into a clandestine state, in the society of the Rose Cross. And it will appear hereafter that Knight Templar Masonry originated in a similar way.

The membership of Royal Arch Masonry are kings and priests. The law of analogy, as well as historic data, points to the fact that the descent of kings and priests into secrecy made the Royal Arch department of Masonry. The descent of the priest took place in 1540, when the Pope confirmed the institution of the Jesuits by a Bull. The priesthood was now poured down from the visible Church into the secret Catholicism with enough of laymen to represent fully the whole Catholic Church. This descent from visibility to invisibility, was powerful and complete. The civil and ecclesiastical powers were moved by them. And Masonic history bears witness to what gigantic efforts they made to control Freemasonry in the interest of the Catholic Church.

At this time Masonry had but three degrees, and Hiram Abiff, the Master Builder, was the undisputed hero of the third grade. The great legend of this degree told of his moral heroism, violent death, and the vengeance executed on his murderers. The stone-masons were taught to honor him. He was idolized because he died sooner than reveal Masonic secrets. They were instigated and encouraged to avenge his violent death on proper persons, traitors and enemies.

The Jesuits now interfered with Masonry, and removing Hiram, the Builder, from the legend of the third degree, for political purposes, put a dead king in his place. This substitute was none other than Charles I, who was beheaded in the days of' Cromwell. And now this same Charles I is the man whose violent death is represented in the degree of Masonry. The Republicans are his murderers, and all good Masons are expected to avenge his death upon them.

Mackey makes this statement: "After the downfall of the house of Stuart, and the defeat of the Pretender's hopes in 1715, his adherents vainly endeavored to enlist Freemasonry as a powerful adjunct to his cause. For this purpose it was declared by those who enlisted in his design, that the great legend of Masonry alluded to the violent death of Charles I.; and Cromwell and his companions in rebellion were execrated as the arch traitors whom the Lodges were to condemn." *Lexicon,* page 215.

The stone-masons, who were mostly Republicans, were incensed to see their adored Hiram removed from the great legend of Masonry, and a king who had never shaken a stone-hammer put in his place. This produced the great schism spoken of in Masonic history, between the Free and the Accepted Masons. The latter class were comparatively numerous and powerful, and effected the transformation of the Order in 1717, after the death of Sir Christopher Wren, the builder of St. Paul's Cathedral and last Grand Master of Operative Masonry. The great schism between the Free and the Accepted Masons, about the Builder and the King, became permanent; for Rebold says: "Such historians as attribute to the partisans of the Stuarts the institution of Freemasonry, and who constantly believe that this allegory portrays the violent death of Charles I., are in error; for it requires but a very limited knowledge of the ancient mysteries to see in Hiram, the Master Workman, the Osiris of the Egyptians, the Mithras of the Persians, and the Bacchus of the Greeks." page 61.

Such quotations prove that the hero of the legend was changed from a builder to a king by the Jesuits and royalists, and the Stuart kings, who were the first kings of Speculative Masonry, and who have left their name and image in the Royal Arch degree.

During the war with Cromwell, Charles I. lost his kingdom and his life. Charles II. in trying to recover the throne of his father, was defeated by Cromwell and fled to France. During his exile the Accepted Masons received him as a king and made him a Mason. He was now a true Masonic king without a kingdom. So was James II., and so were his children, down to the last pretender. They were kings in the Lodge and nowhere else, all being Masons, according to Masonic history. Robinson says Charles II. was a Mason.

Thus the Stuart kings perpetuated their titles in the Lodge, and the claim that the legend of the highest degree then known referred to their murdered ancestor, formed the germ of the present Royal Arch degree. Mackey says, that "before the year 1740, the essential element of the Royal Arch constituted a part of the third degree." *Lexicon*, page 120. Robinson says, that "the Master's degree was formed or twisted to test the political principles of the candidate." So far, all is in perfect harmony.

The Jesuits were still at work down to the time of James II., changing or inventing Masonic forms and symbols. Robinson says, "the Jesuits took a more active hand in Freemasonry than ever. Changes were made in the Masonic symbols, and the emblem worn as the gorget of the Scotch Knight was made to refer to the exiled king." *Proofs,* pages 29—30. Mackey informs us that the element of the Royal Arch existed prior to 1740, and that Dr. Oliver says it is co-eval with the great schism. Well might it be. It was the prime cause of the schism, and was worked by schismatics, and made perfect by the schismatic Lodge of York. (See Rebold, page 102.)

The Royal Arch was first worked by Jesuits with other high degrees in the interest of Catholicism and royalty. It followed in the wake of the exiled kings. It appeared at Arras, in a chapter founded by the young Pretender; and at York was made the highest degree in a Rite of seven, its present place and form.

Thus the descent of kings and priests into concealed existence and operations, gave rise to Royal Arch Masonry. And Masonry was christened the "Royal Art" by Charles II., when the third degree was made to represent the death of his father. Before the end of the first two hundred years after the establishment of the Jesuits, they were quite powerful. The apprehension of the nations caused them to decline. They were banished from England, Portugal, France and Spain, and after the institution was abolished by the Pope, they were forty-one years without legal existence. The decline and fall of the royal house of Stuart, was co-eval with that of the Jesuits. Simultaneously they appear in Masonic Lodges, the common receptacle of all the perishing Orders of the Roman Empire.

## INFIDELITY.

There are many degrees of Infidelity in Masonry, from the mere absence of any acknowledgement of Christ Jesus, to the direct onslaught on his religion, of the "Knights Adepts of the Eagle and Sun." In the Philosophical Lodge of this degree, Father Adam and Brother Truth instruct the candidates to fight against and destroy "the reigning religion," Christianity.

Who put this Infidelity in the Lodge? It was never put there by Christians; therefore it is the work of infidels. The law governing Masonic formations, and common sense, prove that Infidel Masonry was made by Infidels. We proceed to state the facts.

The age which ushered in the French Revolution it is believed, produced more Infidels than any other period in the world's history. A mighty host of them arose simultaneously in Germany and France, all led by such men as Prof. Weishaupt, of Bavaria, the Baronet Nigge, Frederick of Prussia, Mirabeau, D'Alembert, Condorcet, Diderot and Voltaire, who resolved to destroy Christianity and change the civil government. As a failure to accomplish this revolution would be destructive of their lives and property, they chose Secretism as affording the greatest chances of safety and success. They could readily trace the success of

Jesuitism to the centralized despotism of its government, and clearly perceive the general escape of Freemasons from punishment, which they could not fail to rightly attribute to the power of their secret obligations. Many took shelter in the Lodges without delay. But a secret society which would unite the principles of Jesuitism and Masonry, was thought by Adam Weishaupt to be the best for Infidels to use in their perilous undertaking. Barruel states that "in his mind, therefore, he combined the plan of a society which was at once to partake as much as convenient of the government of the Jesuits, and the mysterious silence and secret conduct of Masonry."

Weishaupt was an Infidel. The society he founded was intended to overthrow Christianity as well as civil government. The leading Infidels of the age made a wholesale descent into this secret society, and called themselves Illuminati.

This association is minutely described by both Barruel and Robinson. It originated in Bavaria in 1776; extended rapidly over Germany; appeared at the Masonic Congress at Wilhelms Baden; touched at London, and arrived at Paris, under Masonic forms, in 1787, two years before the execution of Louis XVI. Barruel gives us the information that when the Elector of Bavaria seized the archives of the Illuminati, he found "in the cypher of the Order receipts for making the *Aqua Topana,* the most acute of all poisons, for producing abortion in women, and for poisoning the air of an apartment; also a collection of one hundred and thirty seals of princes, noblemen and bankers with the secret of taking off and imitating all for which the order might, according to circumstances, have occasion." *Memoirs*, Vol. IV, page 266.

The Bavarian monster not only made Illuminism a receptacle for Infidels, but also a place to breed them. The old Infidel was taught the mystery soon; the young were carefully trained. Weishaupt's "Scrutator" was at once the new beginner's companion and seducer, who required of him a confession of his crimes and follies, a record of which was kept, so that his character might readily be destroyed should he ever become the enemy of the Order. Infidel books, lectures and questions schooled him. Kept ignorant of all he wished to know, bound to unknown superiors whom he could not betray, he was bewildered and shackled at every step, till seeming to be ordained like a preacher and to receive sacrament like a Christian, he was called a Priest. Deprived of conscience and manhood, he became a hypocrite. Often a priest, he lived on the Church he was pledged to destroy. While professing loyalty to the throne, he was surrounding it with treason; or while drawing money from the government he had sworn to defend, he was plotting its betrayal into ruin.

Weishaupt directed the Illuminati to capture the Lodges. Dreading the *Aqua Topana* more than Masonic penalties, they obey, and beat the Masons at their own game. They catch the funds of the Lodges, and by a secret within a secret, soon obtain mastery over them. Thus these "evil men and seducers wax worse and worse, deceiving and being deceived."

Barruel records that Nigge "opens the gates of the Lodges from the North to the South, and from the East to the West, to receive the founder of Illuminism." "It crawls from den to den until it attains those of Phillip of Orleans, who, joining the sect with all the adepts of his occult Lodges, gives it sovereign sway over the whole of French Masonry." *Memoirs,* Vol. IV, page 6 and 98.

Illuminism in those days was no less than a Masonic Rite. A Rite was made by adding some secret formation as high degrees to the first three degrees of Masonry. Mackey and Barruel both admit that the Illuminati did this. And Rebold, who is not given to dodging, has put Illuminism down among Masonic Rites; thus, page 230, "Rite of the Illuminati of Bavaria, by Prof. Weishaupt, 1776."

From all this the intelligent reader cannot but admit it proven that Masonry became the receptacle of the Infidelity of Europe.

## KNIGHTHOOD.

Knighthood within the Empire of Charlemagne and the Cæsars, was a military Order. But the military, being only an arm of the civil power, it was also a civil Order. Knights in the beginning were soldiers. Between the time of Charlemagne and the Crusades, they were an Order of nobility in the State, and the cavalry of the army. They served as cavalry in the army of Godfrey, who took Jerusalem in 1099. This Order was not in any sense Masonic at this time.

Gibbon says: "The service of the infantry was degraded to the plebeians, and the honorable name of soldier was confined to the gentlemen who served on horse back, and were invested with the character of Knighthood. The Dukes and Counts who had usurped the rights of sovereignty, divided the provinces among their faithful Barons; the Barons distributed among their vassals the fiefs or benefices of their jurisdiction; and these military tenants, the peers of each other and of their lords, composed the noble equestrian order, which disdained to conceive the peasant or burgher as of the same species with themselves. Their sons alone who could produce four quarters or lines of ancestry without spot or reproach, might legally pretend to the honor of Knighthood." Vol. II, page 331.

This language of Gibbon shows that the Knights were not a Masonic order at first, but a titled order of the Roman Empire; and being exalted in rank, title and privilege above the commoner or plebeian, formed an Order of nobility belonging to the State. This Order underwent three distinct changes before it became Masonic; and true to the requirement of prophecy, the Catholic

Church had a hand in all three. It was not known by the appellation of Masonry till it was used in the interest of the Catholic Church, during the decline and fall of the royal house of Stuart. It underwent its final transformation when it was conducted under Masonic forms and connected with the first three degrees of Masonry. A previous change had been forced upon the Order by the action of a Catholic council, a Catholic king, and the Pope, which, by suppressing it, compelled it either to go into illegal and secret existence, or die.

The first step into secrecy, however, was occasioned by the great influence over the Knights who fought in the holy wars, and the Bull, *omne datum optimum*. A ring is formed to take advantage of those outside; and a ring within a ring is formed to take advantage of the outer ring. Acting on this principle, some Knights formed an order within an order, and directed by the Pope's Bull, admitted the Catholic priests to the immunities of Knighthood. According to Gibbon, "the order of chivalry was assimilated in its rights and privileges to the sacred orders of Priesthood," and in the inside order there was "the strange association of monastic and military life." The Grand Master was a Knight of the Empire and General of the Order, and according to Mackey, "as the vicegerent of the Pope, he was the spiritual head and bishop of all the clergy belonging to the society." *Lexicon*, page 258.

This strange compound of knights, priests and Popery, with military, monastic and secret despotism, took upon itself the distinguishing appellation of Knights Templar. The Order of the Hospital, afterwards called Knights of Malta, being of plebeian origin, the Orders of Chivalry poured headlong into the Templars, to be carried downward to the degraded destiny of secret existence and the Masonic Lodge.

Nevertheless, during two hundred years of legal existence, they had the advantage of the inside ring, and amassed great wealth, lands and manors, with an annual income of twenty-four million dollars. But the bloody failure of the Crusades, and doubtful loyalty of the Templars, with increasing secretism and corruption of manners, hastened their destruction. They were charged with embracing Pantheism, and adopting the forms and mysteries of the Assassins, with whom they were in league; with fighting with the Knights of Malta, and requiring an oath of their initiates inconsistent with the safety of civil government. Barruel states that two hundred Knights Templar testified against themselves that the Order was guilty of Sodomy and infanticide. And he further says that "their depositions declare that the Knights Templar, on their reception, denied Christ." *Memoir*, Vol. II, page 368—9.

Barruel remarks: "Such, nevertheless, are the men from whom the Masons glory in being descended. Yes, and their descent is real. Their pretensions are no longer chimerical; were they to deny it, we should force them to recognize the corrupt portion as their progenitors." Vol. II, page 377.

The change of the Templars from a civil to a secret order of the Empire, took place when the united powers of Church and State moved together for their overthrow. Phillip le Bel, better known as Phillip the Fair, king of France, declared that the suppression of the Order was necessary to the safety of his throne and person. Their great wealth could but tempt his cupidity. The Order of the Templars was suppressed by the Pope and the Council of Vienna, and large amounts of their property were given to their rivals, the Knights of Malta. Phillip le Bel, king of France, burned James de Molay, the Grand Master of the Templars, at the stake. Numbers of the Order were burned alive or hung. Some went to the Hospitallers or Knights of Malta. Many made a deeper descent into secrecy to perpetuate their Order till they could recover their property and civil rank. But civil government throughout the Empire had taken their property, and would not restore the Order.

Barruel says: "After the extinction of their Order, a certain number of criminal Knights who had escaped the general proscription, formed a body to perpetuate their frightful mysteries. To their pre-existing code of impiety, they added the vow of vengeance against kings and pontiffs who had destroyed their Order." *Memoirs*, Vol. II, page 378.

Thus, according to Barruel, went down another Order of the Roman Empire into secretism to rise no more. Mackey says on this point, that the Order was "suppressed throughout Europe, but was not annihilated. De Molay, in anticipation of his fate, had appointed John Mark Larmienus as his successor in office; and from that time to the present there has been a regular and uninterrupted succession of Grand Masters." And again he says that "the Order as it exists in Britain and America, is a lineal descent of the ancient Order." *Lexicon*, page 263—5.

These authors must be set aside, or the descent is proved. The age of chivalry is passed. The Knights of Malta delivered up their island to Napoleon I.; for their end was also to be that they should perish forever, or exist only in the imagery of a Masonic Lodge. The Knights Templar continued to confer the rank and title of Knighthood in secret, for fear of the civil authority, struggling to recover their real rank and title of nobility and their former vast possessions for many years. The following oath is a mark of their continuation:

"In the Lodges of the Knights of Kadosch, after all the oaths, ceremonies and trials, more or less terrible, wicked and impious, three manikins are shown to the candidate, representing Clement V., Phillip le Bel, and the Grand Master of Malta, each attired in attributes of his dignity. The unhappy fanatic is here to swear eternal hatred and death to the three proscribed persons, entailing that hatred and death on their successors in their default. He strikes off the three heads, which as in the degree of Elect are real when they can be procured, or if fictitious, filled with blood. He does this, crying out, 'vengeance, vengeance!'" *Memoirs*, Vol. IV, page 148.

This oath, given by Barruel, proves that the now secret Order is bitter against, and jealous of their old rivals, the Knights of Malta, who prospered long after the Templars were suppressed. The reader will remember that Phillip le Bel and Clement V. burned the Grand Master of the Templars alive, and suppressed the Order. The fact that these two persons were slain in effigy at every initiation, or some helpless victim died, clearly proves continuation.

The same French historian, who was himself an eye-witness to much that he relates, says that this vow of vengeance was executed by the Templars on Louis XVI., whom they, with the help of the Illuminati and other Masons, guillotined, and upon great numbers of the Catholic clergy, whom they assimilated, drowned in the Seine and burned alive.

According to Bernard, the candidate of this degree as worked in American Lodges, is required to swear "to look upon the Knights of Malta as our enemies; to renounce forever to be in that Order, and regard them as unjust usurpers of the rights, titles and dignities of the Knights Templar, into whose possessions you hope to enter." *Light on Masonry,* page 295.

Much more proof of the vital connection between Templar Masonry of today and the Knights Templar of former times might be given, but we forbear. The reader may easily judge whether the Templars were an innocent and persecuted Order, or whether for their crimes they were driven into secrecy by an avenging God, and by England, France, and all the civilized powers of the world.

*First:*—Knighthood was a civil and military Order of the Roman Empire.

*Second:*—The Templars were Knights of the Empire, with an addition of Catholic priests, and constituted an Order within an Order. This was the first step of Knighthood in the descent of secretism.

*Third:*—Being deprived of legal existence by the Pope and the civilized nations of the earth, they became a purely secret Order, retaining their title, and striving for the recovery of their lost rank and property.

*Fourth:*—Failing in this, they became a Masonic Order, as we find them today, uniting their sword with the trowel, and James de Molay with Hiram Abiff, swearing to avenge the death of both on the enemies and traitors of Masonry.

CHAPTER VIII. | 163

Though the original Order of Templars was, like its last Grand Master, "given to the devouring flame," yet its title, spirit, connection, imagery and image belong to the Masons, whose society is the receptacle of this, another of the defunct Orders of the Middle Ages.

# CHAPTER IX.

Six kinds of Masonry have now been noticed. The seventh, derived from the stone-masons or Roman Colleges of Builders, is the fundamental Freemasonry of the world, and is known as Blue Lodge Masonry. Rebold says it is the stock into which all other kinds of Masonry have been grafted, and thus admits that pieces of foreign wood have been introduced into the Masonic tree, and have become its branches; and by the same admission informing us that all these branches grow out of the same root, and that root is Blue Lodge Masonry.

According to all Masonic history, this kind of Masonry inherits the heathen mysteries by lineal descent from the Roman Colleges of Builders, and now gives form, name, unity and character to all the Freemasonry of the world; and beyond all this has taught Oddfellows, Orangemen, Pythians, and all the secret family of earth, the nature of Masonic imagery, and how to clothe themselves with Masonic forms.

Many regard the Blue Lodge as the secret continuation of the Roman Colleges of Operative Masons. These Colleges of Builders were an association of architects who, from the infancy of Rome to the close of the sixteenth century, monopolized the public building of the Empire, till this monopoly was destroyed by the introduction of Protestant ideas. A few Lodges of these Builders in Scotland, the Lodge of York, and four Lodges of London, were the feeble remnants of the Roman Colleges at the close of the seventeenth century. These Builders are the Operative Masons referred to in Masonic Rituals of today, whose working-tools are still employed at all the initiations of the Blue Lodge. These initiations are a continuation of the forms used at the introduction of laborers into the Roman Colleges. These laborers obtained recognition and employment by the same grip now used. The slaying of the corner-stones of public buildings by the Blue Lodge is another mark of its direct descent from the Builders of the Empire. There is much historic evidence of this fact, but we will give the reader only one quotation from Rebold's History, page 247. After the most careful examination of the subject, the author says:

"We have found that Freemasonry is the issue of an ancient and celebrated corporation of artists and mechanics, united for the prosecution of civil, religious, naval and military architecture, founded in Rome in the year 715, B. C., by the renowned law-giver, Numa Pompilius."

To issue is to flow out; the issue is that which flows out. Therefore what is here called Masonry must have first existed among the Builders or it could not have issued from them. What was it that thus issued and is now known as Freemasonry? It could not have been the stone-cutter trade practiced by the Builders, nor architecture; for the Lodge now neither practices nor teaches either. It could not have been that civil establishment which they say was derived from Numa Pompilius, maintained by the laws of the Twelve Tables, and continued by emperors, generals, kings and popes. No; time has swept that all away, and it lies in the same grave with the Colleges of Builders. Then what is it? It was the heathen mysteries that issued, and are at the present styled the mysteries of Masonry; because these mysteries were derived from an order of men who were masons by trade and heathens by religion. These mysteries issued in Masonic forms, with a Master Mason called Hiram, occupying the place of one of the gods, as hero whose worship the mysteries celebrate. The old legend of the death and resurrection of heathen gods is found in the third degree of modern Masonry, and is an ancient heathen invention, instead of modern origin. It may be found among the Colleges of Builders, an order which originated among heathens.

CHAPTER IX. | 167

The third degree cannot be an invention of the four Lodges of London in 1717, if it existed in the operative Lodges of Builders before that time. We have shown elsewhere that "Charles I., king of England, who was beheaded in the days of Cromwell, was placed by the adherents of his house as the hero of the third degree, instead of Hiram Abiff; that Charles II. was made a Mason and frequented the Lodges;" and that James II. was represented on the gorget of the Scotch Knight. Now, Prof. Robinson records the fact, on the 21st page of his "Proofs of a Conspiracy," that in the days of these kings, "the Ritual of the Master's degree seems to have been formed or twisted from its original institution." It must have been in existence or it could not have been twisted. Again he says: "The Revolution had taken place, and King James, with many of his most zealous adherents, had taken refuge in France. But they took Freemasonry with them to the Continent, where it was immediately received by the French." Pages 24—5. Further, after the degree of Scotch Knight had been added to the first three, he says: "But it is certain that in 1716 this and still higher degrees of Masonry were much in vogue in the Courts of France." Page 26.

These kings had much to do with Masonry, and Masonry as much to do with these kings. The first was crowned in 1625, and the last died in 1701. Hence the third degree existed among the Builders before the birth of the Blue Lodge, and issued from the bowels of one of the Orders of the Roman Empire, along with the germs of higher degrees.

Robinson wrote on the spot where these events transpired more than eighty years ago. He is fully sustained by Rebold and Mackey, and in substance by Barruel. In these men we have the concurrent testimony of the adhering and seceding Mason, of the Protestant, Catholic and infidel, and of the Scotch, French and American writer, that these things are so.

The Builders, from whom the Masonic mysteries issued, originated in an age when the heathen mysteries everywhere abounded. They were heathens themselves when the legislative act of Numa Pompilius gave being to their Order, for he was second king of Rome.

There is another way by which Masons show the identity of heathen mysteries with their own. They claim, and seem proud of the fact, that wherever mysteries are found, whether among the heathens of Asia and Africa, or in the Lodges of civilized countries, they are essentially the same. This is a strong proof of common origin.

As the mysteries were first among the heathens, and of heathen origin, they existed of old under various names and modifications, but of one type. The secret character of the ceremonies, and the oaths and death-penalties by which they were guarded and maintained, produced a great degree of uniformity in every age and every clime. For instance: the mysteries of Adonis-Tammuz, Bacchus, and those of the

CHAPTER IX. | 169

third degree of Masonry, are precisely of the same type. Not only are they claimed to be identical by Masonic authors themselves, but they are essentially the same.

The mysteries were instituted by the heathen priests for the secret worship of the gods and the religious training of the worshipers. A short extract taken by Mackey from Warburton, and given below, shows that none understand this truth better than the Freemasons.

Mackey says: "Warburton's definition of the mysteries is as follows: 'Each of the pagan gods had (beside the public and open) *a secret worship* paid to him, to which none were admitted but those who had been selected by preparatory ceremonies called *Initiation*. This *secret worship* was termed the *Mysteries*.'" *Lexicon*, page 313.

From this it is clear that the mysteries of Adonis was the worship of Adonis; the mysteries of Bacchus, the worship of Bacchus; and other mysteries the worship of those heathen gods whose names they bore.

Each of these ancient mysteries had a hero, and each hero was a god. Sometimes he was a demon, and often he was the spirit of a dead man. But whoever or whatever the hero deity was, he was the representative of the seasons, Summer and Winter, and the forces of Nature which produce them. Consequently the myth on which the mysteries were based declared he had been killed, or had received a deadly wound and had recovered, in order to make his history correspond with the phenomena of the seasons. The glory and strength of the Sun at the Summer Solstice, with the life and beauty of Spring and Summer; and again the departure of the Sun for the Winter Solstice, with the consequent suspension of the productive forces of Nature, and death of the vegetable kingdom in Winter, were the archetypes of the heathen mysteries. The death and resurrection referred to in the secret worship, were inherent principles in Nature, and not in the god who was hero of the mysteries. In the mysteries the reference was a myth to make the hero represent Nature. The approach and departure of the Sun with increased and diminished heat, making the change in the Seasons, caused that luminary to be worshiped, and the hero god who represented him in the mysteries to be worshiped also.

The story of Adonis and the Boar illustrates the nature of heathen mysteries. This myth informed the worshipers of the Sun, that Adonis was a beautiful youth with whom Venus fell in love, and both dwelt together for a season. But one day, while hunting on Mount Lebanon, he was wounded by a boar, on the source of a river, which, from this occurrence, was named the river Adonis. The water of this stream was said to be colored with blood at a certain period every year. Hence the Syrian damsels made an annual lamentation for wounded Adonis.

Initiations into the mysteries of Adonis, Mackey states, "were funeral in their character." The men suffered or seemed to die like the god, and the women who wept for the wounded hero, prostituted themselves like Venus. It was thus that they celebrated the mysteries of Nature, and the return of Adonis to the bed of Venus.

According to the highest authority, the Tammuz of Ezekiel is the Adonis of the Syrians, and the word is rendered by Adonis in the Vulgate. The prophet Ezekiel, when in the Spirit, beheld and heard the secret things the ancients were "doing in the dark, every man in the chambers of his imagery;" and saw the "women weeping for Tammuz," and witnessed the men with their faces toward the east "when they worshiped the *Sun* toward the east." Upon the inspired account of the mysteries of Sun-worship, contained in the eighth chapter of Ezekiel, Milton has the following beautiful lines:

> "—*Tammuz came next behind,*
> *Whose annual wound in Lebanon allur'd*
> *The Syrian damsels to lament his fate*
> *In amorous ditties all a Summer's day;*
> *While smooth Adonis from his native rock*
> *Ran purple to the sea, supposed with blood*
> *Of Tammuz yearly wounded: the love-tale*
> *Infected Sion's daughters with like heat,*
> *Whose wanton passions in the sacred porch,*
> *Ezekiel saw, when, by the vision led,*
> *His eye survey'd the dark idolatries*
> *Of alienated Judah.—*"

Mackey is not afraid to assert plainly that Masonry is a continuation of Sun-worship. His language is: "The number '12' was celebrated as a mystical number in the ancient systems of Sun-worship, of which it has already been said that Freemasonry is a philosophical development." Manual of the Lodge, page 100. And again:

"The Master and Wardens are symbols of the Sun; the Lodge of the universe or world; the point also is the symbol of the same Sun, and the surrounding circle, of the universe; while the two parallel lines point not to two saints, (the saint Johns,) but to the two northern and southern limits of the Sun's course." Page 57.

The Master is the great symbol which represents the Sun; the Lodge is the symbol of the world; therefore the dramatic performances of the Lodge are the similitude of the seasons, with the Sun at the two northern and southern limits of his course, that is at the Summer and Winter Solstices, when he is farthest from the equator. Indeed Mackey and Oliver and other Masonic authors explain the various steps in the Lodge-rites and arrangements, by allusions to the phenomena of the seasons, and references to corresponding features in the ancient worship of the Sun. Masonry is, in fact, Sun-worship. Hiram, the hero of the third degree myth, is killed; and following the Sun god-type, every Master Mason is killed also, after the manner of a myth, knocked down, rolled up in a blanket, and buried; then, after having been planted together in the likeness of the Sun-god's death, they rise like Mithras, Bacchus or Adonis, the hero-gods of heathen myths.

The archetype of the mysteries being found in Nature is what makes them so much alike, a change in the hero, making a change in the name only. Adonis being hero made the mysteries of Adonis; Bacchus, being hero, made the mysteries of Bacchus; and a Master Mason being hero made the mysteries of Masonry. The Builders, who began their career under the mysterious tutelage of Bacchus, after a while changed the original hero for a Master Mason and fellow-craftsman, Hiram of Tyre, the widow's son, who assisted at the building of Solomon's Temple. When Hiram was thus exalted, he had every attribute and qualification of a heathen deity. He filled the place the heathen gods has filled, and was the same in kind as they. Were they dead men? he, too, was a dead man. Were they made heroes of the myths and mysteries?—so was he. Was their worship secret, and guarded by oaths and death-penalties?—so was his. Were initiations into their mysteries assimilated to the myth, and as Mackey says, "funeral in their character?"—so are the initiations under Hiram, the candidate being struck, wounded, killed and buried, like Hiram in the legend. Was the hero Adonis the symbol of the Sun in Sun-worship?—so was Hiram the symbol of the Sun in two relations, as Master and hero. Mackey says that in the Lodge "the

Master is the great symbol of the Sun." Then how much more the representative of the Sun-god is he whom "the great legend of Masonry" makes Grand Master of the Lodge and hero of the myth at the same time. In these relations Hiram is a god of equal rank and dignity with Adonis and Bacchus. A brief quotation from Rebold's history will serve to show how well Freemasons understand this truth.

On page 392, he says: "A very limited knowledge of the history of primitive worships and mysteries is necessary to enable any person to recognize in the Master Mason Hiram, the Osiris of the Egyptians, the Mithras of the Persians, the Bacchus of the Greeks, and the Atys of the Phrygians, of which these people celebrated the passion, death and resurrection, as Christians today celebrate that of Jesus Christ."

Rebold can see in Hiram the Master Mason, the nature and fullness of four heathen gods. We can see at least the perfect measure of one heathen deity in Hiram the Master Mason, and that as initiations are assimilated to the story of his sufferings. Masons celebrate his passion and death as the symbol of the Sun in this way. The design of the mysteries was not then to represent the state or transformation of the dead, as some have written, but to represent the phenomena of the different seasons of the year, and to symbolize the Sun, which seemed to heathen minds on a cold wintry day, to be the wounded hero of the scene.

Masonic writers are those who have grouped their own Hiram with heathen gods, and they have done it more than once. They are the men who inform us that Masons celebrate his passion and death as Christians celebrate the passion and death of Jesus Christ. These writers do not seem to be afraid to confirm the statements of seceders who, leaving the Lodge in horror, assert the same things; nor do they hesitate to admit that their mysteries were the secret worship of pagan deities, and are essentially the same in every age and country.

It certainly appears strange that Mackey should point out the eighth chapter of Ezekiel and twenty-fifth of Numbers, and join with Christian poets and commentators in maintaining that the Adonis of the Syrians was the Tammuz of Ezekiel; and stranger still when he quotes Calmet and Faber to prove that both were identical with *Baal Peor.*

What can it be that makes Freemasons so apparently eager to acknowledge the identity of heathen mysteries with their own, unless it be the fact that this identity is true and so boldly prominent as to preclude concealment?—or what is it that induces them to point us, with a view to establish their claims, to those scriptures where God Jehovah has so unmistakably condemned them, except it be that species of insanity which has sometimes been known to follow the taking and faithful keeping of Masonic oaths.

Now if it be true that Hiram the Master Mason fills the place and has the attributes of a heathen god, so manifestly that all who are in the least acquainted with heathen worships and mysteries, can recognize in him "the Osiris of the Egyptians, the Mithras of the Persians, the Bacchus of the Greeks," and many other such gods; and if it be true that Masons celebrate his passion and death, like heathens paying divine honors to their deities, or as Christians paying divine honor to Christ the crucified, then, beyond question, Hiram is a god. If it be true that Masonry is a development of Sun-worship, and "the Master and Wardens are the symbols of the Sun, the Lodge the symbol of the universe or world;" and if it be true that the ceremonies of the Lodge are essentially the same as the worships and mysteries of Adonis, Tammuz and Baal Peor, then the moral character of heathen gods and heathen mysteries is the moral character of Freemasonry. This is a logical necessity.

When we search in the Bible for the real character of heathen gods and worships, we find that their gods are devils and their mysteries eminently sinful. Deut. xxxii: 17: "They sacrificed unto devils and not to God; to gods whom they knew not." Here it appears heathen gods and devils are all one. Upon the same subject the Psalmist says: "They joined themselves to Baal Peor, and ate the sacrifices of the dead. They sacrificed their sons and daughters unto devils." Psalm cvi. St. Paul says: "The things which the Gentiles sacrifice they sacrifice to devils and not to God; and I would not that you should have fellowship with devils. You cannot drink the cup of the Lord and the cup of devils; you cannot be partakers of the Lord's table and of the table of devils." 1 Cor. x: 20, 21. When Masons celebrate the passion and death of Christ at the table of the Lord, and then celebrate the passion and death of Hiram in the Lodge, they break this command of the apostle.

The devil has usually been named after the heathen god through whom he deceived mankind, or from the image chosen to represent him, as in the case of Baal. For the Baalzubub of the Old Testament is Beelzebub the prince of devils in the New; and devil, satan, and Beelzebub are used interchangeably by Christ and the Jews. Matt. xii: 24—27. Devil and serpent have been used synonymously ever since the devil, through a serpent, deceived Eve.

The valley of Hinnom, or Tophet, where heathens and apostate Jews worshiped fire-gods and devils amid the cries of burning children and the sounding drums, was the symbol of hell with the faithful Jews of Bible times. The learned Smith, in his "Bible Dictionary," says: "The later Jews applied the name of this valley Ge Hinnom, Gehenna, to denote the place of eternal torments. In this sense the word is frequently used by our Lord: Matt. v: 29; x: 28; xxiii: 15; Mark ix: 43; Luke xi; 15." The Lord Jesus, knowing all things, beheld in this place of suffering devils, and fire, more of the nature and elements of hell than of any other place.

Again, the learned Smith of London informs us, that Adrammelech and Anammelech, the gods of Sepharvaim, were the male and female powers of the Sun. Dictionary, page 37. Sepharvaim is the same as Sippara, a city situated on both sides of the Euphrates above Babylon. Berasus styles it "a city of the Sun," and it bore an inscription which, translated, read "Sippara of the Sun," because the Sun was the chief object of worship there. The Bible assures us that the wicked Jews "burnt their children in the fire to Adrammelech and Anammelech, the gods of Sepharvaim." 2 Kings, xvii: 31.

The worship of these Sun-gods was identical with that of Moloch, the fire-god of the valley of Hinnom, the symbol of hell. Is this the Sun-worship of which Mackey tells us "Freemasonry is a philosophical development?" Are the Master and Wardens "symbols of the Sun, and the Lodge of the world?" Are Masons still compelled to believe the story of Hiram's death by violence without evidence and against evidence, and then simulate that death in every initiation? Do they still lament the annual wound, and grope for God about the tropics? Masonic authors and the Scriptures of truth both bear witness that the Masonic gods are devils and their mysteries sinful, "the mysteries of iniquity;" that Masonry gropes for God, but finds the devil.

The host of heaven and the powers of nature were the earliest objects of heathen adoration. In the mysteries of solar idolatry they worshiped the Sun, and an intermediate being who was hero of the myth and symbol of the luminary. He might be an honored ancestor or a fellow-tradesman, but was always some cherished personage dear to the people who made him their Sun-god. They could then pay him divine honors, simulate his death or deadly wound, receive his mark, and rejoice in his recovery, as the representative of the Solar orb. Summer and Winter in their correspondence to the Sun's greatest declination from the equator, were the archetypes to which the mysteries still conformed when the hero was changed. Adonis, Mithras, Osiris and Bacchus were so many heroes, but the mysteries conforming to the archetype were not materially modified. It was the exercise of no new power in the Roman College of Builders, when they changed the hero Bacchus, of their mysteries, for a builder and called him a Master Mason, in order that the worshiped and the worshipers might be of the same trade. Nor was it an unusual act, when they substituted a myth for the true biography of Hiram, that his death and history might coincide with the false biography of

Bacchus and of the boar-torn Adonis, and thus conform to the archetype of the mysteries.

There was a grand effort made in the seventeenth century, by the royalists of England in connection with the Jesuits, to change once more the hero of the mysteries from a Builder to a King, from Hiram Abiff to Charles I. They lamented the violent death of Charles by the democrats far more sincerely than that of Hiram by the three ruffians. During the conflicts which desolated England in this century, the Puritans and democrats were opposed by kings, royalists and Jesuits who, seeing the adaptability of Masonry to their purpose, crowded into the secret meetings of the Masons, and the Lodge soon became an engine of politics and war. This influx of royalty and Jesuitism, with the attempt to displace the god of the Lodge, gave rise to "the great schism between the Free and Accepted Masons." The Builders contended for the old hero, and the Accepted Masons declared that the third degree portrayed the violent death of Charles I. and the destruction and restoration of the monarchy. Or to use the language of Mackey, they said that "the great legend of Masonry alluded to the violent death of Charles I., and Cromwell and his companions in rebellion were execrated as the arch traitors whom the Lodges were to condemn."

This is what Robinson calls twisting the Master's degree "from its original institution;" and adds, "for it bears so easy adaptation to the death of the king, to the overturning of the venerable constitution of the English Government of three Orders by a mean democracy, and its re-establishment by the efforts of loyalists." *Proofs*, page 21. The mysteries now symbolized the British Government which caused the formation of high degrees, and in the plaintive language of Rebold, "gave to this time-honored institution a character entirely political."

It seems but fair that if the Builders who were architects had a right to change the hero of their mysteries to an Architect, the Kings of England and the royalists had an equal right to change him to a King. But these schismatic Masons did not stop till they had made the destruction and restoration of the British Monarchy the archetype of the mysteries, and the bleeding and headless king became more the symbol of monarchy than of the Sun, or Winter and Summer. Thus, as Robinson says, the Master's degree was twisted from its original institution, for "it bears so easy an adaptation to the death of the king, to the overturning of the constitution of the English Government of three degrees by a mean democracy, and its re-establishment by the loyalists."

The attentive reader will at once see that when civil Government had the same bleeding symbol as the Sun, and held the same place in the mysteries when the Sun and the forces of nature had been so long enthroned receiving the homage of the nations, from that moment men paid divine honors to civil Government according to the strictest forms of heathen worship. It is thus that men worshiped the Beast through the heathen ritual. The worship of civil Government beginning in England, one of the ten kingdoms of the Beast, spread rapidly over the other nine with all their subdivisions and colonies.

The Worship of the Beast is the worship of civil Government, and is clearly unearthed in the thirteenth chapter of Revelation. There Masons may find their own bleeding symbol, their own type at worship, and their marks.

If the Government of England was overthrown by "mean democracy," or democrats, and restored by royalists and Jesuits, so the whole government of the Roman Empire was overthrown by the irruption of the northern barbarians, and was restored by Popes and French kings. This is the archetype; and the Beast which had "one of his heads as it were wounded to death, and his deadly wound was healed," is the bleeding symbol of the destruction and restoration of this Empire. Here our commentators are agreed.

The Beast is the last hero of the mysteries, the last successor of the bleeding Adonis and the headless king. The fact that he is a symbol holding an intermediate position between his own image and marked worshipers, the power which he represents, and the fact that he had a deadly wound apparently, and was restored to life again,

CHAPTER IX. | 183

shows that he is of the purest type of heathen hero gods whose mysterious worship symbolized the Solar year, and, according to some, the apparent diurnal motion of the Sun causing day and night. Thus Rebold says, page 392: "In an astronomical connection, Hiram is the representation of the Sun, the symbol of his apparent progress; which appearing at the south gate, so to speak, (when Hiram is first struck by Jubela) is smote downward and more downward (struck again by Jubelo) as he advances toward the west, which passing, he is vanquished (slain by Jubelum) and put to death by darkness, but returning he rises again, conqueror and resurrected."

Nothing can be seen in all this of the power or the time when "the dead shall be raised incorruptible and we shall be changed;" but we can see in the Beast of bleeding and deadly wound, "the Osiris of the Egyptians, the Mithras of the Persians, the Bacchus of the Greeks," the Hiram of the Masons, the headless king of the Jesuits, and the Devil-worship referred to in the Scriptures. This Devil-worship the Scriptures expose, showing its type, symbols and language. If Masonry had no worship of this type, no symbol of this character, no marks of similar import with the forehead mark of Mithras and the ivy mark of Bacchus, then it would not correspond with the prophetic symbols. Then the prophecy must fail, its tongue must cease, and knowledge must vanish away; for it is now more than a hundred and fifty years, at least, past the time required for the fulfillment, and nothing else has appeared in the Roman Empire to meet the conditions of the prophecy, but Masonry. Unless Masonry possessed these marks, mysteries and other coinciding characteristics, it would not be Masonry, and could not be the Image of the Beast.

The reader will now perceive the fact that the Civil Order of Builders or Roman Architects poured its oaths, death-penalties, its mysteries, worship and gods, with all its membership and vital forces, its name and working tools, into Speculative Freemasonry. No longer depending for existence on its civil establishment or material purposes, it became a secret Order, and sought safety from extinction in becoming the bowels of its own offspring.

The act which confirmed the change of Operative to Speculative Masonry is before us, and indicates continuation and transformation. It was passed by the St. Paul's Lodge in 1703, adopted by the four Lodges of London in 1717, and afterwards by all the Lodges of the world.

*"Resolved:*—That the privileges of Masonry shall no longer be confined to Operative Masons, but be free to men of all professions, provided that they are regularly approved and initiated into the fraternity." Rebold, page 56.

This resolution may be considered more as the effect than the cause of the transition, for men of all professions were already inside the Lodges, and had been there for a long time in great numbers. Thus sunk another civil Order of the Roman Empire into the secret or Image Empire of Masonry, to rise no more forever.

# CHAPTER X.

The data and proofs which sustain the facts of history we have presented may be found elsewhere in these pages, and are now before the reader. Only a condensed statement of these facts can be given in this place.

1. Sun-worship is based on the annual course of the Sun and his daily revolutions which produce in their order Summer and Winter, day and night. The annual wound of the Sun-god who represented the Solar year, symbolizes the Winter Solstice with diminished light and heat. The death and funeral of the Sun-god who represented the day, symbolizes the setting and departure of the Sun under the earth at night, and the utter destruction of the light of day.

2. Hiram, the Master Mason, is a Sun-god. Masons speak the truth when they say he is "a Symbol of the Sun." The flight of Hiram Abiff from the south gate or noon, to the west gate or Sun-set, and being killed before passing the east gate or sun-rise, is a representation of the Sun descending from the glory of noon to

the darkness of night and apparent death, before his morning resurrection. As the flight and death of Hiram is simulated by every Master Mason, initiations are the celebrations of the death and resurrection of Sun-gods and the Sun.

3. The Jesuits "twisted" Sun-worship so as to make it celebrate the death and resurrection of Monarchies, Empires, Orders of nobility and defunct dynasties, giving birth to high degrees. Governments were now worshiped in the same manner as the Sun, which was Beast-worship. Sun-worship was changed to Beast-worship by that secret arm of Catholicism, the Jesuits, showing an intimate vital connection of Masonry with the Catholic Church. Being employed in that form by Catholics to resurrect the monarchy, destroyed by Cromwell with great success, it was in the interest of the Catholic Church that monarchical government was first placed in the mysteries as an object of worship, receiving divine honors. Through all the forms of Sun-worship, "the Beast whose deadly wound was healed," is the symbol of slain and resurrected monarchical government. In Sun-worship and Beast-worship the symbol and the power symbolized are both slain and resurrected. We have shown that the latter was derived from the former. Not content with all this, the Jesuits worked in Masonry till after the middle of the eighteenth century, run the chapter of Arras, and one in the Jesuit College of Clermont at Paris, being the

unknown superiors of their own Masonry, and overriding other forms of the institution. The connection of the secret arm of the Catholic Church with Masonry, is too evident, and should never be denied. The connection of Masonry with the Roman Empire is still more evident and tangible.

We have traced seven portions or kinds of Masonry to seven Orders of the Roman Empire, and shown their points of juncture by the facts of history. We have retraced these seven orders from their origin to the time of their descent into the Secret Empire, where, receiving character from the mysteries, they were united under Masonic forms and denominated Freemasonry. This institution belongs to the Roman Empire by birth and permanent residence. It is the likeness and contemporary of the revived Beast or Roman Empire. The titles and Orders of the Empire are continued in Masonry. The institution is the near relative of the Beast; it is connected with him and has sprung from him.

The relationship of the Beast and Masonry is like that of Adam and Eve. When the Lord took one of Adam's ribs and made Eve, the man said, "This is now bone of my bone and flesh of my flesh." If this one rib establishes a close relationship between the first pair, is not the relationship equally or more close between the Beast and Freemasonry, when it took seven ribs of the former to make the latter? And as the rib and flesh of Adam

CHAPTER X. | 189

died as parts of Adam and lived as Eve, so some of the Orders of the Roman Empire died as Orders of that Empire and live as Orders of Masonry. Some of them went down alive into the Secret Empire, retaining their names, titles and emblems.

Masonry was made out of the substance of the First Beast, and is related to the Second Beast with two horns like a lamb. This connection is essential to the fulfillment of the prophecy. If Masonry is not in some way connected with the Roman Catholic Church and the Roman Empire, it cannot be the Image of the Beast; for the Image is connected with both the symbols which represent the Church and the Empire. The plan and animus of the Image is derived from the one and it belongs to the other. According to the language of the symbols the Beast is in the possessive case; the Image is his image, the image of him and belongs to him, and is associated with him in worship by his marked worshipers.

The slain and revived Empire—the Church or Papal Hierarchy, and Freemasonry, are three arch criminals whose pictures God has taken in a group that we might recognize them each by the others. All are related to each, and each to all, like the members of a family, or, like father, mother and child. The discovery of the picture of one leads to the discovery of the rest, with threefold evidence to prove the identity of each. The same relationship and likeness that exists between the criminals also exists between their pictures, and this meets the requirements of the prophecy.

The Roman Empire contains three kinds of government in connection with three co-existing powers, civil, ecclesiastical and Masonic government, exercised by the Empire, the Church and Freemasonry. The thirteenth chapter of Revelation is a comprehensive picture of the triple Empire with explanatory notes. The three prophetic symbols are pictures of three co-existing governments or criminal powers. These criminal powers may be known by their crimes and distinguished by their characters.

One look at the Empire and its picture reveals the fact that Masonry is the Image-power. Masonry has all the attributes of an image; the others have not. It is the quality of an image to represent something; Masonry has this attribute. In other words, Masonry has the attributes of an image because it is a mass of imagery. Everything in it represents something that is not in it. The Lodge represents the world, the Master and Wardens the Sun, initiations the death of Sun-gods or monarchies. According to the "Masonic Chart," the Priest informs the Masonic King that his Scarlet Robe is "an emblem of imperial dignity," his Crown "an emblem of royalty," and himself "the representative of a King." Webster says imagery is representation. Masonry is representation; therefore it is imagery. The Royal Arch

Mason, Wilson, intimates the same thing when he says: "Here oral expression and *imagery* addressing the ear and eye mould the true Mason."

So lively is the imagery of the Blue Lodge, that if witnessed by the people of the seventeenth century, they might readily suppose that men calling themselves Entered Apprentices, Fellow-crafts and Master Masons, with squares, compasses, mallets, chisels, hammers etc., were stone-masons of the old type preparing to build St. Paul's Cathedral. Masonry is the imagery of the nobility, kings, emperors, governments, priests, mitres, crowns, orders and powers of the Roman Empire, and therefore in wisdom and righteousness was named the "Image of the Beast." None but that God who called Cyrus by name so long before his birth could have thus so appropriately and significantly named Freemasonry.

When we compare Masonry with the Roman Empire, the Beast and the Image, in all their parts and attributes, a hundred correspondences appear between them and confirm the truthfulness and wisdom of the name—"Image of the Beast." The things of Masonry correspond to things of the Empire. The titles, Orders and institutions of one correspond to those of the other. The correspondence of the Beast with the Image is very clear; that of Masonry with the Empire is equally clear. For the Image and Masonry are the image of the Empire and the Beast, and all must correspond to each other. The Empire and the Beast being the same, must surely correspond; and the Image and Masonry being the same, must also correspond. This inter-relation and mutual correspondence between each with all and all with each, may be fully demonstrated by studying the following lines of comparison:—

1. Compare the Beast with the Empire—the Image and Masonry.
2. Compare the Empire with the Beast—the Image and Masonry.
3. Compare the Image with the Beast—the Empire and Masonry.
4. Compare Masonry with the Beast—the Empire and the Image.

This twelvefold correspondence, where the parts and attributes of each correspond so perfectly with those of all, prevents any possibility of mistake. There is a full jury of correspondences, the unanimous verdict of which must be "Guilty."

If all the particulars of this multitudinous and complex correspondence should be written, it would overflow the wants and memories of mankind, and the world could not contain the books that would be published.

There is also a religious correspondence between Masonry and the Empire, like that between the Image and the Beast. Masonry takes the emblems, military weapons and working-tools of well-known institutions of the Roman Empire, and makes them the symbols of Masonic religion. The symbols of Masonry are sacred things. Religion and morality is preached from each of them as from a text of Scripture. What they teach is explained in the Lectures of the Lodge. Masonry has never acknowledged any other guide to holiness or heaven.

What are these symbols, and whence came they? They are derived from the Roman Empire. They are emblems, weapons and tools which belonged to the civil, military and mechanical Orders of that Empire, and are symbols of the Orders from which they were taken. Masons who use a particular class of symbols take the name of the Order from which the symbols of that class are borrowed. There is thus such a religious correspondence between Masonry and the Empire as to keep the eyes of every Mason fixed on the Beast.

It may now be seen without difficulty that the correspondences between Masonry and the group of prophetic symbols are numerous and often idolatrous. The data are tangible and proximate. The argument is cumulative, ever increasing in volume and power. The truths which support the position we have taken are kindred truths whose reciprocal action so mutually sustain each other that they can not be torn asunder, but must bear witness through all time, that the Image of the Beast is the symbol of Masonry.

With such data it matters little where the argument begins, the same result must follow. If we begin by saying the ten-horned Beast which Daniel saw is the fourth kingdom that should arise, the Roman Empire appears as the fourth kingdom, and is, therefore, the ten-horned Beast. This cannot be denied without resisting the strongest evidence and the ablest commentators; for the wise have long known that the Empire is the Beast, and have often counted the number of his name. From the moment it proved that the Empire is the Beast, there is twofold evidence that Freemasonry is his Image. The latter is the inevitable sequence of the former. If the Empire is the Beast, then Masonry is the image of the Empire, and therefore the Image of the Beast. If the Image of the Beast is the image of the Empire, then Masonry is the image of the Empire, and is, therefore, the Image of the Beast.

There are religious affinities between the Beast and his Image. They are objects of the same idolatry and united in worship. If the Beast is the Empire the worship of the Image is connected with the Empire, because it is connected with the Beast. The worship of Masonry is connected with the Empire, and therefore with the Beast. If the Worship of Masonry and of the Image are both connected with the worship of the Beast, then their worship is the same idolatry, and Masonry and the Image are the same thing; or, in other words, the Image of the Beast is the symbol of Freemasonry.

CHAPTER X. | 195

The thirteenth chapter of Revelation is a representation of three governmental powers which prevailed in the Roman Empire. The civil and the Catholic powers are the first and second, and the image-power is the third. Masonry is an image-power, and the third kind of power in the Empire; therefore it is the image-power represented by the third symbol, the Image of the Beast. More proof might be added; less would be sufficient to sustain our point.

It will be hard for Masons to believe this prophecy while they continue to practice the crimes which fulfill it. It was hard for the civil and Catholic powers to believe the prophecies concerning themselves, and they did not while shedding the blood of the martyrs. It was hard for the Jews to believe that the Son of Mary, whom they crucified, was the Christ. It may be hard for many to believe that Masons are the marked worshipers of the Beast and his Image, because being true it portends much evil to Masons and to men. But it is impossible to change the facts of Roman history which support the foregoing arguments and deductions, or to modify the symbols which God has chosen to represent those facts.

It may be difficult for some to believe that the secret Lodges of our day, like the Jews, reject the crucified One. It may be difficult and unsavory for many to believe that loved ministers, relatives and friends have received the marks of the Beast and are worshipers of his Image; for it indicates that such must drink of the unmixed wine of the wrath of God. But these are facts, nevertheless, however unpalatable they may be.

The civil, Catholic and Masonic powers are the same in number, order of succession and character as the symbols which represent them, and are connected with, and flow into each other in the same way. Masonry has a religious and literal connection with the Roman Empire. The idea that the civil might be governed by a secret Empire was a Catholic conception. Sun-worship was changed to Beast-worship that Protestant England might be restored to the Church of Rome. The first high degrees, including the Royal Arch, were made in the interest of the Catholic Church. They were full of the imagery of the Roman Empire; and the Empire was the Beast.

If Masonry fulfills all the numerous and intricate requirements of this prophecy without one failure, what more evidence need heaven give or men demand that this institution so wide-spread and popular is the Image of the Beast.

There is strength in the fact that Masonry belongs to the Roman Empire by birth, relationship and residence; much in the fact that it is the easily-recognized likeness of that Empire; and more in the fact that it has all the necessary attributes of an image, to justify the wisdom of the name, "Image of the Beast." The Empire, the Beast and the Image are three that bear witness to these truths. And history, prophecy and type are three that bear witness that Beast-worship, Masonic-worship and Devil-worship are the same.

Some have expressed the opinion that when the judgment or mercy of God shall have broken the nightmare that has fallen upon the Churches, when times have changed, and interest no longer blinds the eyes of men, then shall the remarkable and accurate fulfillment of this prophecy be treasured up among the evidences of Christianity.

# CHAPTER XI.

Two lines of comparison have been drawn: one between Masonry and the Roman Empire; the other between Masonry and the Beast, the symbol of that Empire. A third comparison remains to be drawn between Masonry and its own symbol, the Image, in reference to matters not dwelt on before.

The Beast received power "to make war with the saints, and to overcome them." The Image received a similar power "to speak, and to cause that as many as would not worship it, should be killed." It is a logical necessity that the Image should be like the Beast. Both received power over the lives of their subjects. It is vital to our purpose to prove that Masonry possesses the same power over the lives of its members that is ascribed in Scripture to the Image.

If we examine the authentic expositions of Masonry, we will find that in its chosen mode of existence and organic structure, it has provided itself with power to kill those of its subjects who refuse to worship it. There are oaths of murderous intent connected with every degree in every Rite of the Masonic system, presaging death to every penitent Mason who renounces his oaths and repents of his sin. In order to obtain the benefits of Masonry, the candidate must go at least to the third degree. To attain this position he has three times bowed in abject worship before the Masonic altar at the Master's feet; three times sworn allegiance to Masonic government; and three times on oath delivered up his life into Masonic hands for security. In a religious sense, these oaths may be considered as acts of devotion required by the god of Freemasonry, wherein the candidate three times lays down his body upon the Masonic altar, to become a living sacrifice in the vengeance of the Masonic god, if he should tell to the world the mysteries of his worship. In another sense, these oaths may be considered as part of a business transaction, equally binding on both the contracting parties. The Master Mason has received from the Lodge, among other things, the knowledge of Masonic secrets; and in return, the Lodge has taken his throat, his heart and his bowels as security that he will discharge his obligations and never betray its secrets to the world. Through the Chapter degrees, in each succeeding oath, he delivers his life as a hostage, into Masonic hands. In all these degrees, the death-penalty is laid against some part of the candidate's body; his throat, heart, bowels, hands, tongue, breast, skull, brains and other parts. There is also in each degree, a corresponding sign, having deadly reference to the penalty, and to that part of the body against which the penalty is laid. Thus: if the penalty is to have the throat cut, the sign is to draw the right hand across the throat, as if in the act of cutting it. If the penalty is to have the left breast torn open and the heart and vitals taken from thence, the sign is made by drawing the hand from the left breast across with quickness to the right, as though in the act of tearing out the heart and vitals, thus referring to that penalty. These signs, referring to death-penalties, being ever afterwards used and recognized by Freemasons as valid, prove that they are living penalties, of abiding force, and constitute a life-destroying power in the Masonic organism.

But this fatal power of Masonry over the lives of its members, is not confined solely to the body, nor to this state of existence. It pretends to reach the soul, and into the future world. The two-horned Beast, or Church of Rome, has ever pretended to a penal power over the souls and the eternal life of those who forsook his worship; in consequence of which, the anathemas and excommunicating Bulls of the Pope are dreaded by his subjects as the sentences of damnation from the Judge of all the earth. The Image received its life-principle, and its power to speak and execute the death-penalty upon its refractory subjects, from the two-horned Beast; so that we may reasonably expect to find in the Image the same daring assumption of punitive authority over the temporal and eternal life of its worshipers, as that manifested by the Pope. Even here Freemasonry is found to fulfill its marvelous symbol to perfection. In many of the higher degrees, the penalty of repentance and renunciation is laid against the soul and the eternal salvation of the candidate, in the most fearful manner. For instance, in one degree, he takes in his hand a human skull, and imprecates upon himself the sins of the person to whom it once belonged, in addition to his own; then from it he drinks in wine a double damnation. In another degree the penalty of disloyalty is, "May I be Anathema Maranatha;" that is, accursed at the Lord's coming.

Again. The speaking Image had something to say, and what it said, had an effect. It could speak and cause murder; or speak in defense of its conduct, when it committed murder. There is something in Freemasonry to correspond with these characteristics of the Image. Freemasonry can speak and cause the death of him who betrays its secrets. The despotism of Masonic government gives it power to speak. The oaths that every Freemason has taken to obey, forbids them to rebel. The darkness of the night they have chosen for their meetings, and the organized secrecy which conceals all they do from the world, make it impossible to know when or on whom they intend to commit injury or murder. If they should be suspected, they can defend themselves by arguments such as are drawn from the nature of their society. They can say to him who resolves to worship Freemasonry no longer, but reveals its secrets: "Sir, we never invited you to join us. You swore at our altar that you came of your own 'free will and accord.' You asked our confidence, and we gave it to you. You asked for a knowledge of our secrets, and swore in the presence of God and under the penalty of death, to keep them. We revealed them to you, and trusted you on the security of your life. You asked for the benefits and advantages of our Order, and you have enjoyed them all. You have received at our hands, our lamb-skin or white apron, 'an emblem of innocence and the badge of a Mason. It has been worn by kings, princes and potentates of the earth, who never have been ashamed to wear it. It is more valuable than the diadems of kings or the pearls of princesses; more ancient than the Golden Fleece or Roman Eagle; more honorable than the Star and Garter.' You have dishonored the badge of your profession, and violated a contract to which you yourself was a voluntary party. You have injured, insulted and betrayed us; and according to Masonic law, you shall and ought to die."

Thus speaks the Image in our midst, and so strong seems the argument, that Masons from without are saying of him who forsakes their altar, "It is right he should be killed, and we will help to kill him;" while

Masonic voices from within respond, "Amen, so mote it be." There is much in the relations and organic structure of Masonry, both to enable and to impel it to kill. If the Masonic Priesthood were consulted, would they speak the truth, they must say, "Our operative ancestry, and the Eleusinian Fathers of our religion, took the lives of those who betrayed them. We are all sworn to observe the ancient land-marks. This man, who laid down his body a living sacrifice upon our altar, has betrayed us, and there he should be immolated. 'We have a law, and by our law he ought to die.'" The Entered Apprentice can say, if consulted, "He has betrayed us; but we have taken security on his throat. It is time to cut it." The Fellow-craft can say, "We have as good as taken a judgment note on his heart, including the right of way. Let us tear it out." The Master Mason can say, "He has acknowledged the validity of our death-penalty by giving the sign of it. We have seen him drawing his right hand over his bowels, where the penalty of our degree is laid: he has imitated the cutting out of his own bowels. We will hold him to his bargain. The traitor has the sign; he shall have the substance."

The Royal Arch Mason can say, "In passing through our preparatory degrees, we have taken a Masonic lien on his hands, his tongue and heart, and have marked him on the left breast, as a sign of the covenant he made with us. He swore to us the right to cleave his skull and scorch his brains. The only way to preserve our secrets, our interests and our honor, is to kill him and say, that all he has told the world are lies." The Knights of Kadosch will say, if inquired of, "He must be killed; for we have sworn to take vengeance on the traitors of Masonry. We must kill him to save ourselves from treason and perjury." The Knights of the Eagle must say, "If any person divulge our obligations, we are 'bound to cause his death, and avenge the treason, by the destruction of the traitor'" The Illustrious Elected of Fifteen must say, "The penalty of our degree is, to have our body opened perpendicularly and horizontally; and we have taken the obligation 'to be ready to inflict the same penalty on all who disclose the secrets of this degree.'" The Elected Knights of Nine must say, "We have sworn in the presence of Almighty God, that we will 'avenge the assassination of our Worthy Master Hiram Abiff, not only on the murderers, but also on all who may betray the secrets of this degree.'"

Thus the man who, in the lower degrees, has delivered himself up to be destroyed, in case he betrays the fraternity, finds in the higher degrees, men who are sworn to kill him if he does. It is vain and foolish to say that such a wicked looking institution as this will not kill. It is absurd and false to say it cannot kill. Therefore, Masonry is like the Beast, and answers to God's description of the Image.

If a Phrenologist were to examine Masonry, he would say, "Its Destructiveness and Secretiveness are very large." The Physiognomist would say, "I see something in its countenance that says, 'I am a liar, a thief and a murderer.'" The Statesman would say, "Terror is the foundation of the Masonic superstructure. I see frightful references to death-penalties, used as signs of recognition between its members, and are acknowledged to be a just claim to Masonic protection and the discharge of Masonic obligations. The thing seems planned to destroy its traitors and its enemies. Even its playthings are swords and poniards, coffins, ropes, human skulls and skeletons, bleeding hearts and severed heads; and its entire framework seems red with the elements of slaughter." The Divine might say in truth, "I see in Freemasonry the speaking Image of the Beast. It is a true likeness of the Dark Ages, and the shadow of the Crusades, the armies of the Beast. It is the troubled Ghost of the Roman Empire who, in the days of his flesh, crushed the spirit of freedom and slew the martyrs of Jesus. Masonry in its rituals, lectures and references, utterly ignores the true Christianity of the Middle Ages, and takes no knowledge of the fact that such men as Jerome and Huss ever suffered and died; or that fifteen millions of human beings were slain, who sought but liberty of conscience and the rights of man. It is fitting that such men should not be named amid the excitement and hilarity of Masonic play; for those who originated Speculative Masonry, the Priests and Kings, were the very men who slew the martyrs. It is proper and natural then, that Masonry should leave the saints and martyrs of those times unnamed, and mutter the names and titles of their murderers, while assuming all the pageantry and pomp of princes, kings and emperors, deacons, priests and popes, whose titles are interwoven throughout the different rites of the system. From all these considerations, it appears that Masonry is both a murderer and the image of a murderer; the moral likeness of the Beast, and the express image of his person."

We need scarcely say, that according to ancient history, those who celebrated the ancient mysteries enforced their death-penalties against such as betrayed their secrets; or that Rebold says, page 299, that an Operative Mason murdered a Bishop to prevent the escape of Masonic secrets, and that some now take the obligation upon them to bring traitors to punishment, agreeably to the rules and usuages of the ancient fraternity. Neither is a reference to Morgan, Abbot, nor to Miller, really needed here; nor yet the murdered Pichard and Priest, who lost their lives for publishing "Jachin and Boaz." nor Noah Smith, of Vermont, who lost his life for republishing it, nor Captain Ariel Murdock, who lost his life for circulating it; neither Richie of Philadelphia, nor Gavitt of Ohio; neither Hunt, of Boston, who was murdered for revealing Masonic secrets; neither the Emperor Alexander, who, it is said, was assassinated for suppressing Masonic Lodges in Poland and Russia; nor all those nameless victims which swell the numbers of the murdered dead. These instances may show that Masonry does do what we have shown it has power to do, to kill its subjects.

We have taken our stand on the murderous character of the Masonic organism itself, to prove that it can speak, and cause that as many as will not worship it shall be killed. In this respect it is both like the Beast, and equally corresponds with God's description of the Image.

It is the public opinion of our times that Masonry maintains a monopoly of all unpunishable murders. When a man murders a Freemason in cold blood, the murderer dies, and there is none to save him. But if a Mason kills a man, Masonry saves the murderer from the law, and practically says, "A Mason shall not die for any cause, but for the violation of Masonic law, and by Masonic hands. The civil law and the profane shall not blast his character nor take his life." Thus murders are duplicated; and sounds of wailing and anger are heard in the land. We should remember that law, long violated, will at last avenge itself. Then will men say, "If a Freemason cannot be hung for killing another man, then no other man shall be hung for killing a Freemason. 'With what measure you mete, it shall be measured to you again.'" Oh! that these dangerous and perishing men would regard what may be their last call to repentance; the earnest warnings that disturb the air throughout the nation, and the united voice of the good and true of every Church, sounding like the voice of the Third Angel, saying, "If any man worship the Beast and his Image and receive his mark in his forehead, or in his hand, the same shall drink of the wine of the wrath of God."

The second reason which enables us here to identify Masonry as the thing symbolized by the Image is, that both are extraneous inventions of man, connected with, or attached to the civil compact. The Beast was a wicked government: the Image was made *"to the Beast,"* and worshiped in connection with him. Hence, the Image was the governmental likeness of the Beast, attached to him by men for idolatrous purposes. Masonic history informs us that certain higher degrees became "entirely political," and raised fallen dynasties, and were used as a Church instrumentality. The lessons of experience have also taught mankind the same truth.

It is no small proof of the identity of Masonry and the Image, that each holds the same relations to Government as the other; that each is an artificial appendage and governmental likeness of the Beast, attached to the civil compact. Wronged and wondering thousands are waking yearly to the knowledge of the fact, that Masonry is an idolatrous appendage to society, and a supplement and forgery attached to the Charter of Man's Inalienable Rights; which changes the working of the Charter, destroying equity, reversing the decisions of justice, defeating the will of majorities, changing the normal relations of trade, and producing inverted action in all the civil compact.

The third reason that enables us to identify Masonry as the thing symbolized by the Image is, that they are both idolatries. The idolatry of Masonry consists in, first, the worship of heathen deities. The universal claim of Masonry is, that it possesses the heathen mysteries; the mysteries of Osiris, Eleusis, Bacchus, Adonis, and of the Druids, etc.; and that all these mysteries are substantially the same. Albert Mackey says, that the Roman Colleges of Builders, from which modern Masonry descended, were worshipers of Bacchus; and the modern Lodge, as if mistaking itself for a College of Builders, still celebrates the mysteries of the worship of Bacchus, as they did. This is a religious idolatry.

The idolatry of Masonry consists in, second, the civil worship of the Beast; or that kind of homage which baser minds are wont to pay to such notable persons as emperors and kings, popes and cardinals, and other rulers of the Beast; or the adoration of his kingdoms, armies, invincibility and ferocity; or the homage paid to Mammon, the love of wealth, honor and position, which the depraved and covetous are doomed to feel. This civil kind of worship is idolatry, as certainly as "covetousness which is idolatry," and well agrees with the opinion of commentators, who believe that the worship of the Beast was of a civil character. In this sense, Freemasons give as much evidence as men can give, that they worship the Beast, when they love his moral character and all his governmental principles; when they assume the titles and royalty of its emperors and monarchs; and when they display and admire the tinselry and pageantry of the nobility and priesthood of his realm. Freemasons have made their institution the image of the glory and honor, as well as of the blasphemy and ferocity of the Beast. Therefore, Freemasonry worships the Beast; that is, renders civil homage to him. There has always been such an idolatrous connection between Masonry and the government, as frequently enables the members to gain those positions in Society, whose titles they assume in the Lodge, or such other positions as they desire. Thus the Beast is worshiped through Masonry, its Image. The Beast was always the enemy of God, and the destroyer of His people; yet from civil motives, perishing thousands worship him and commit sin, blind to the terrors of their approaching doom.

The third kind of Masonic idolatry is the worship of itself. Its entire literature, standard, periodical and forensic, is full of self-laudations. Its songs sing of

"Masonry divine;" its prayers pray for blessings through "the secrets of our [Masonic] art;" its god is a "Grand Architect," like a Freemason Builder; and its heaven is a "Grand Lodge above;" where their god presides as "Grand Master." Thus Masonry worships itself and its own likeness, in its god and its heaven. No wonder; for it denies the Son, and has not the Father. Christians worship a triune God, the Father, Son and Holy Ghost; and these three are one. Masonry being a threefold idolatry, worships Bacchus, the Beast and his Image; and these three are one; for Bacchus is one of the gods of the Beast, and included in his general worship.

Masonry is the assemblage of every principle of the Beast, and is the Image through which he is worshiped, that has "power to speak, and to cause that as many as will not worship it shall be killed."

# CHAPTER XII.

It is a sad duty which we now have to perform, to prove that the symbols of Masonry and the marks of the institution, which its members place on their own persons, are marks of the Beast. Our heart trembles when we contemplate the body of evidence which proves this; evidence that seems too strong when we gaze into the faces of men who have received those marks. Though we had before looked upon them as dangerous and perishing, now we forget that they are dangerous and remember only that they are perishing; and that the Third Angel pronounces upon them the severest penalties of the Divine Law: "If any man worship the Beast and his Image, and receive his mark in his forehead, or in his hand, the same shall drink of the wine of the wrath of God, which is poured out without mixture into the cup of His indignation; and he shall be tormented with fire and brimstone in the presence of the holy angels, and in the presence of the Lamb, and the smoke of their torment ascends up for ever and ever; and they have no rest day nor night, who worship the Beast and his Image, and whosoever receives the mark of his name."—Rev. xiv: 9, 10, 11.

There is an idolatrous connection existing between the Beast and his Image, which is acknowledged in Scripture, wherever they are mentioned; a connection similar to that which existed between the god and the image of the ancients. Commentators are of opinion that there is an allusion to the ancient forms of idolatry, when the Beast and his Image are used as symbols of modern idolatry. Therefore, a knowledge of the former is the best means of understanding the latter. The first witness we shall bring to prove the nature of ancient idolatry, is Benson; not for his opinion as a commentator, but as a witness to a historic fact. He says:

"We must remember that it was customary among the ancients for servants to receive the mark of their master; and soldiers, of their general; and those who were devoted to any particular deity, of the particular deity to whom they were devoted. These marks were usually impressed on their right hand or on their forehead, and consisted of some hieroglyphic characters; or of the name expressed in vulgar letters, or of the name disguised in numerical letters, according to the fancy of the imposer."

For the same purpose the second witness brought is Scott, who says:

"It was a fashion in St. John's time, for every heathen god to have a particular society or fraternity belonging to him; and the way of admitting any into these fraternities, was first, by giving him some hieroglyphic mark in the hand or forehead, as that of the ivy leaf to the fraternity of Bacchus." Barnes says they were marked "on the hand or elsewhere."

Now the Beast occupies, in modern idolatry, the place of the god of the ancient idolatry; and Masonry occupies that of the image of the god. The relative positions in which symbols of Masonry and the Empire are placed, prove this. If it can be ascertained how, where, and by whom the marks of the ancient idolatry were given and received, then shall we find how, where, and by whom the marks of the Beast are given and received. According to the authorities quoted, the marks were impressed on the person, and consisted of some hieroglyphic mark or name in vulgar letters, or the same disguised in numerical letters. These marks were given by the fraternity that worshiped the god, and were received at the time and place of worship, by the candidate, during his initiation into the society of worshipers, and were indicative of the peculiarities of the god. Masonry as foreseen by the prophet in its Beast-worship, acts in exact conformity to all this.

Now the Beast is the substitute in modern idolatry for Bacchus, Osiris, Ceres, or any other god, demi-god or deified hero, in the system of ancient idolatry. St. John has foretold, therefore, in what he has written, that as the ancient god had an image, so the Beast should have an image; that as the god had a fraternity who worshiped the god and his image, so the Beast should have a fraternity who should worship the Beast and his image; and that in exact conformity to the ancient idolatry, this fraternity should impress marks upon the naked person of every candidate they received into the society which worshiped the Beast, and that the marks they impressed or otherwise imposed, should be marks of the Beast, the god they all worshiped. As we have given full proof that the Roman Empire is the Beast and Masonry the Image, therefore it is at the time and place of worship, in the Masonic Lodge, the idol's temple, that the candidate should receive the mark of the Beast. In conformity to this prophecy, Freemasons mark their candidates in this time, place, and manner, and blind to what they are doing, call it "marking," "mark," and "the mark."

While meditating on those Scriptures which refer to these idolatrous marks, and aware that commentators who had brought forward the mode of marking in the ancient idolatry to explain the mode of marking in the modern idolatry, had not shown anything in the latter to correspond with the mode of marking in the former, the thought forcibly presented itself to our mind, that there was something in Masonry that we had not noticed which fulfilled those Scriptures. On examination of Bernard's

"Light on Masonry," and Richardson's "Monitor," we found that in the plainest possible manner Freemasons practice the ancient mode of marking; and that the word *"mark"* is emblazoned on the face of Masonry revealed. We find it used seventy times, in its various relations, in Richardson's description of the Mark Master's degree alone, which takes its name from its Book of Marks, and the number of marks which are given and received in this degree. Each man receives three marks; a private mark in his right hand, a general mark of the degree, and a mark impressed on the naked breast with the engraver's chisel. Thus a Lodge of one hundred men receives three hundred marks of the Beast; and as if left to the sport of a pitiless destiny, they call themselves "Mark Masters." According to Bernard, the Knights of the Christian Mark receive a blasphemous mark in red letters on their forehead. In the Thrice Illustrious Order of the Cross, the candidate swears, "I do now, by the honor and power of the *mark* of the Holy and Illustrious Order of the Cross, which I do now hold to heaven in my *right hand* as the earnest of my faith, in the dread presence of the Most Holy and Almighty God, solemnly swear and declare that I do hereby accept of, and forever will consider the cross and *mark* of this Order my only hope."

It is not too much to say that Masonry is the only institution which is at once a *fac simile* of ancient idolatry, and of the worship of the Beast, as described by St.

CHAPTER XII. | 217

John. We shall now pause for the purpose of bringing up another matter, as a basis for our concluding argument on the marks.

Commentators have long since shown that in prophetic style the ten-horned Beast is the Roman Empire, and cannot refer to anything else. In every modification of the symbol, whether it be found in the writings of Daniel or John, the Beast is distinguished by his ten horns, an unerring mark of the ten kingdoms of the Roman Empire.

*Second:*—Of the chain of symbols recorded in the seventh chapter of Daniel, the ten-horned Beast is the last in the series, and the latest in time. It is well known that the last of that mighty chain of Empires, extending from the Euphrates of the Tiber, was the Roman Empire.

*Third:*—If the Beast was dreadful and terrible, and strong exceedingly, the Empire was also dreadful and its arms invincible.

*Fourth:*—Did the Empire appear on earth at least seven hundred years before Christ? and in some modification, it is likely to exist to the end of time? In prophecy, the Beast appears before Christ, and having no successor, connects His advent with His final reign.

*Fifth:*—Does the ten-horned Beast of Daniel and John make war with the Saints and overcome them? and is he an enemy of God and His people? So has the

Empire done and been. Christ suffered under Tiberius Cæsar and Pontius Pilate; and an Idumean subordinate beheaded the Baptist, and killed James, the brother of John, with the sword. Paul was brought the second time before Nero; and the people of God underwent ten persecutions from the pagan Beast, before he was converted to Christianity. And after he was baptized and taken into the Church by the two-horned Beast, he drank deeper of the blood of the martyrs than he had ever done before.

*Sixth:*—It is a distinguishing mark of the ten-horned Beast, that his number is 666, and that this 666 is also the number of a man. This circumstance and this number distinguish the ten-horned Beast from all other beasts. The distinguishing number of the Roman Empire is, also, 666, and this 666 is also the number of a man. This circumstance and this number distinguish the Roman Empire from all other empires. We may notice some of the data which have enabled those who are wise to "count the number of the Beast."

The infantile name of the Roman Empire, which was the true name, was *The Latin Kingdom,*—*"He Latine Basileia."* This was the name it bore when Daniel saw it rise out of the sea in prophetic vision; and this was the name it bore in Greece, before Rome destroyed Alba. But after Rome became the capital, the people were called Romans, after the city and its founder, Romulus. Similar circumstances gave to the realm its first name, thus

CHAPTER XII. | 219

subsequently changed. The name of the founder of the Latin Kingdom was Lateinos. The language spoken by this monarch and his subjects, was the Latin language; his people were called Latins; and his kingdom was called the Latin Kingdom. This is the kingdom to be numbered; and this is its real and prophetic name, which it first bore in its infancy and afterwards resumed in its age. The Italians were again called Latins by the Greeks, after the division of the Roman Empire. And Lateinos is the man to be numbered; for this name appears on the people, realm and language of the Empire.

Before the introduction of figures by the Arabs, the letters of the alphabet were used as numerals, just as certain letters of the alphabet were used as numerals by us; thus, XVII=17. The numerical values of the letters which were required to spell a name, when added together like our figures are added, gave the number of that name. When this rule is applied to the Greek letters which spell The Latin Kingdom,—*"H(e) Latine Basileia,"* they make the exact number 666; and when the letters contained in the true Greek form of Latinus,—*"Lateinos,"* are taken at their numerical value, they also make the prophetic number 666. Here is something like demonstration. The number of the Beast is the number of a man, "and his number is six hundred threescore and six,"—666. The Beast and the man have the same number. The number of the Latin Kingdom is also the number of a man, its founder, "and his number is six hundred threescore and six,"—666. The Empire and the man have the same number. The Greek letters are used, because John received the Revelation in the Greek language from Jesus. It is a remarkable additional circumstance that the Hebrew name of the same kingdom, "Romiith," should also contain the number 666.

If Irenæus in the second century, could number the Empire and prove it to be the Beast, by sufficient evidence, each subsequent century has added something to its weight. Rome has since resumed its Latin name, and the Latin language has become the religious language of the Empire. Since then, the sixth head has been wounded to death and healed, and ten kingdoms have shot up to crown the Beast with horns. And last of all, as if there was not yet sufficient proof, Freemasons have fulfilled their destiny by making an image of the Empire; and instituting a ritual and liturgy to worship the Beast. There is no Empire but that of Rome, which contains a living man-made image of itself; and there is no other symbol but its own, of which the prophet said an image should be made. Thus as the ages pass away, the fated Empire fills its symbol, giving to each age new proof that it is the Beast; while Freemasonry in the same manner is furnishing abundant evidence that it is his Image.

It is a logical necessity that if the Empire is the Beast, then marks of the Empire are marks of the Beast.

## CHAPTER XII. | 221

The marks of the Beast are of two kinds. The first kind of marks are those which the Empire has impressed upon the Church and secret societies, by the operation of a natural law. The second and most sinful kind of marks are those of an idolatrous character, which secret societies make in connection with the civil and religious worship of the Beast.

A very plain instance of the first kind of marks is to be seen on the Catholic Church. It is universally admitted by Protestants, that it was the paganism of the Empire that corrupted the Church. Mr. Campbell says:

"Papal Rome has borrowed much from pagan Rome. Old Rome had her *pontifex maximus,* her purgatory, priests and priestesses, her victims and 'hosts.' She had her lustral water, as modern Rome has her holy water. She had her vestal virgins, as her descendent has her nuns. She had her Pantheon, as modern Rome has her Vatican; and in the niches where stood the gods of the Dragon, now stand the saints of the Roman Draconic Lamb."

All these things are marks which the Empire left upon the Church. So also is the despotism of the heathen monarchs substituted for the republicanism of the primitive Church; and the secretism of the Eleusinian and other heathen mysteries of the Empire are substituted for the example of Him who said, "In secret have I said nothing." So great was the change thus produced on the Church by the idolatry, mysteries, secrecy and despotism of the heathens, that her symbols, False Prophet, Man of Sin, etc., prove that she became masculine. The Virgin was transformed into a Beast,—a "he" Beast with two horns like a lamb. And will not Masonic domination over the Protestant Church, and the practice of idolatry and mysteries by her members, transform her into something "he," which like the Man of Sin cannot be reformed, and therefore must be destroyed?

Masonry, taking the Empire for a pattern, contains within itself all the marks or characteristics of the Empire; and other secret fraternities, taking Masonry as a pattern, have many second-hand marks and characteristics of the Empire. These marks, which the Empire seems naturally to impress upon her institutions, may be considered as the least sinful of all the marks of the Beast.

The Societies of the genus Masonic, which possess these characteristics, are each an image of the Beast. But in some of them the image is very partial and imperfect. It is perfect only in the institution of Freemasonry proper. This may be illustrated by reference to the ancient forms of idolatry. The image of the national god or chief deity of the country or locality, was erected in every temple, place and country where the god was worshiped. The image was variously made of gold, silver, stone and wood, and in different periods and countries; the form, size and execution being modified according to the wealth, intelligence and artistic taste or skill of the fraternity who worshiped the deity it was intended to represent. These fraternities were the men who made and received in their persons the idolatrous marks of their god. So likewise, the secret societies of our day are so many images of the Beast, more or less perfectly made, depending on their origin, object, power and extent; and the members of these fraternities are the very men to make and receive the marks of the Beast. Acting in harmony with the prophecy, and observing the true forms of idolatry, they make millions of marks; some impressed upon their minds and souls, perhaps never to be removed; some impressed upon their persons with swords, chisels and other sharp instruments; and some made by the pressure of the thumb-nail on the finger. The signs of death or marks of their obligations are made on the breast, throat and forehead, and on other parts of the body, against which the penalties are laid; and the signs or marks of recognition and fellowship are made in the right hand. Some are made in hieroglyphics, and some in letters or figures; while others, called marks by the giver and receiver, consist of insignia or badges. Some are spread abroad on buildings, merchandise and currency; and others are used as a basis of teaching and symbols of religion.

There are secret societies or forms of Masonry for almost every conceivable purpose: some for the use of the

Catholic Church; such as the monastic orders, Nuns and Monks, Jesuits and Inquisition: some for the cause of Protestantism; such as the Know Nothings, Orangemen, and American Protestant Association: Trades Unions, which Rebold says sprung from Operative Masonry, to secure a monopoly of trades: some for brigands on land, and others for pirates on sea: some for the purposes of revolution, war and temperance: and others for farmers and men in other callings; some for Colleges and nobility; others for the lower classes, and adapted to the poor; and still others expressly for women, and some even for children. All this vast idolatry was caused by a Church whose sins and secrecy, idolatry and mysteries had transformed her into a male Beast. He it was that first conceived the idea of a Secret Artificial Image Empire, and planned the vast system of modern idolatry constitutionally pertaining to it; "saying to them that dwell on the earth, that they should make an image to the beast." "And he had power to give life to the image of the beast;" life to perform the functions of a mighty secret organization, and to make the marks of the Beast of whom and to whom the image was made, upon his many millions of worshipers. He also employed its secret forces in the government of the Roman Empire; took Masonry into the Church, and the Church into Masonry; and in order that the worshipers of the Beast and his Image might be known from the "profane and cowan" world, and control the commerce of the nations, "he causes all, both small and great, rich and poor, free and bond, to receive a mark in their right hand, or in their forehead; and that no man might buy or sell, save he that had the mark, or the name of the beast, or the number of his name."

Operative Masonry was a monopoly of stone-cutting and building; that is, one trade. The various Trades Unions which sprung from it, are monopolies of other trades. Speculative Freemasonry, which originated from the same source, is the monopoly of all branches of business, professional, mercantile and mechanical, and every other department where there is any power to be gained or money to be made. All other secret societies, true to their generic instincts, are monopolies of some department of human industry and interests.

The men who have agreed to these monopolies, are bound to sustain each other in preference to all others. To secure this support and keep it among themselves, they have certain marks by which to recognize each other. Now, reader, can any man who has no mark or sign of the death-penalty in his forehead, nor sign in his right hand, and who has no marks of any monopoly whatever, be a successful business man? He has not a clear ring nor a fair fight, and unless God helps him the man who has the marks of the Beast will come out ahead in the battle of life.

There is another circumstance which gives the man who has the mark a great advantage over all other persons in buying and selling. It is a principle in secret societies, in the very worst as well as in the best, not to injure nor interfere with each other's property nor interests. They form a covenant not to wrong or steal from the fraternity, nor take each other's life. Part of the Masonic obligation runs thus: "I will not wrong this Lodge nor a brother of this degree, to the value of a cent, knowingly myself, nor suffer it to be done by others, if in my power to prevent it."

This is Masonry; and this same kind of covenant is found in every fraternity of the genus Masonic. Even the fraternities of robbers and murderers have it. The mark of the Beast is the sign of the league and covenant they have made. Though this covenant is one with death, and this league is one with hell; yet he who can show the mark and make the sign, secures thereby the safety of his person and property. Thus when a Mason has the mark of the Beast in his forehead and right hand, and puts the square and compasses on his merchandise, he places himself and it under Masonic protection. Masons have covenanted not to injure him; and his property is safe from Masonic rapine. As all successful robbers belong to some of these fraternities, and often too many; and as there is no protection from Masonic rapine but Masonic law; and so of all other secret societies; therefore, the men who have not the marks of the Beast, are plundered without redress, by the robbers of all grades, who swarm in these fraternities. Not only so, but the mark secures for the property of a Mason the quickest sales and highest prices; while the property of others is subject to delay and depreciation. The following extract from another Masonic oath will serve to illustrate this point:

"I furthermore promise and swear, that I will caution a brother Secret Monitor, by sign, word or token, wherever I see him doing, or about to do, anything contrary to his interest in buying or selling. I furthermore promise and swear, that when I am so cautioned myself, by a brother Secret Monitor, I will pause and reflect on the course I am pursuing. I furthermore promise and swear, that I will assist a brother Secret Monitor, in preference to any other person, by introducing him to business, by sending him custom, or in any other manner in which I can throw a penny in his way." *Richardson*, page 92.

There seems to be a design in Masonry and in all its branches, that "no man might buy or sell, save he that had the mark, or the name of the beast, or the number of his name."

Freemasonry is the plainest image of the Roman Empire of any of the secret family. It is not only a general image of the Empire, but also an image of its several parts, jointly and separately. The marks which Freemasons make, idolatrously referring to the Empire, are also the plainest of all other secret marks. They not only refer to the Empire in general, but to some part of it in particular. Each department of Masonry makes marks of that department in the Empire, of which it is the image. The age of the different departments of Masonry, takes the same order as that of the corresponding departments in the Empire.

It is universally admitted that the first three degrees, or Blue Lodge, are the oldest departments of Masonry. The Blue Lodge is the image of the Colleges of Builders, instituted by Numa Pompilius, 715 years before Christ. The religion of the Blue Lodge is still older, having been brought into Italy by Romans, who were initiated into the Grecian mysteries of Eleusis and Bacchus. Thus the gods of the Leopard became the gods of the Beast, and were incorporated, by Rome's great lawgiver, into the College of Builders. The religion of these degrees is purely heathen, both in its origin and character. Its grips, signs, secrecy, its death-penalties and markings, prove it to be the express image of the Eleusinian and Bacchanalian mysteries. This heathenism has been so strictly guarded down to the latest times, that no Mason at prayer in the Lodge, can ask anything of God in the name of Jesus Christ, without violating Masonic law, and laying himself liable to Masonic discipline. The oldest department of Masonry is a representation of an early period of the Empire.

The Chapter has since been added to the Lodge and is a representation of the governmental department in a later period of time, when the civil was subject to the ecclesiastical power. The Chapter is a representation of the kings, priests, governors and government of those times. Still the blue of the Lodge is mingled with the scarlet of the Chapter. The Lodge is fundamental to all other Masonry, as Building was fundamental to the Empire.

The Orders of Knighthood in the Masonic system, are placed above the Chapter; so that the candidate must pass through the Lodge and Chapter, before he can become a Knight. This circumstance would prove that these Orders were subsequently added to the two former departments, even if Rebold had never told us that they were a late invention of the Jesuits in France. The case here is similar to that of the Lodge and Chapter; for these Orders of Masonic Knighthood are the exact image of the Orders of Knighthood previously existing in the Empire. Those Orders existed in, and belonged to the Armies of the Crusades, and continued to multiply till the beginning of the nineteenth century. At first they were composed exclusively of Roman Catholic Chivalry, and being military Orders, they swore to defend the Christian religion with their swords. They were mostly created by Emperors and Kings; were regulated by statutes, and sometimes received pensions from the government. The following quotations are from the

"Cottage Cyclopædia," relating to the Knights of the Empire. They were to be well armed; "they were to protect widows, maidens and children; relieve the distressed, and maintain the Christian faith." The oath which some of them took, was, "You shall also swear to maintain and defend all ladies, gentlemen, widows and orphans;" and another obligated them to "maintain the cause of God and the ladies."

The Masonic Knight swears like the real Knight, and according to Richardson's "Monitor of Freemasonry," takes the following oath: "Furthermore do I promise and swear, that I will wield my sword in defense of innocent maidens, destitute widows, helpless orphans, and the Christian religion." The Masonic Knight assumes the title of the real Knight, dons his military costume, draws his sword, and swears to perform his work. One might suppose that when this pretended Knight had risen from the altar where he had vowed, if he possessed the spirit and truth of the Catholic chivalry of the Crusades, he would draw his sword, go down to the Blue Lodge, cut off the heads of all he could find, for rejecting Christianity which he had sworn to maintain, and the women whom he had sworn to defend; and be ready to lead a crusade against all infidels, as did Peter the Hermit. Thus that part of Masonry, which is the image of the heathen Builders, is heathen; and that part which is the image of Catholic Christian Knighthood, is Catholic Christian.

Though it can be proved that the same Jesus who is rejected in the Lodge, is blasphemed by the Knights, and Masonry is shown not to harmonize with itself, yet its different departments will be found to harmonize in forming a perfect image of the Empire.

In bestowing marks of the Beast on the candidates, the members of each department of the Image Empire, impose on the candidate, the mark or marks of that department of the Empire, of which they form the image, into which he is being initiated. The stone-masons of the Blue Lodge are not presented with a scarlet robe, nor a crown, but with a mallet and chisel, or some other instrument suited to stone-cutting or building. Neither is a Knight presented with a mallet and chisel when he swears to fight for the Christian religion and the ladies. When the Masonic aspirant enters into that department of Masonry which is a representation of the military and chivalrous department of the Empire, he is presented with a sword; not that he is expected to keep his oath by fighting the Blue Lodge or anything else unchivalrous and unchristian; but he is expected to claim and accord the privileges, title and honors of a Knight, don his military costume, draw his sword, and stand the very image of an Order of men who used to fight.

It must be remembered, however, that there is more in Masonry than is in the Empire; while everything that is in the Empire is in Masonry, there is nothing wanting to make the Image perfect. Masonry is like a theatrical representation or work of fiction founded on real history; the history may all be found in the fiction, but the fiction is not found in the history.

The candidate for Masonic Knighthood is marked with the sword, the symbol of the military power of the Beast. He is surrounded with swords; they are placed under his knees and hands, and he swears upon them; and at the charge of the Knights, when he drinks the fifth libation, their points are presented towards, or pressed against his neck and bosom. We are not dependent upon this, however, to prove that all Freemasons have marks of the Beast engraven or impressed on their persons, and otherwise made in their forehead and in their right hand.

The three symbolic degrees and the three preparatory degrees of the Chapter, are fundamental to all Freemasonry. Their forms prevail through and over everything Masonic. All Freemasons, in passing through these degrees, have marks of the most frightful idolatrous significance, impressed, stamped, cut in, or engraven on their persons, by the working-tools of the Colleges of the Builders of the Empire; proving that whether we take it in a literal, logical or prophetic sense, they are marks of the Beast, and marks impressed by the fraternity who worship him. After a careful examination of the subject, Albert Barnes says:

"The word here rendered 'mark,' occurs only in one place in the New Testament, except in the Book of Revelation; Acts xvii: 29, where it is rendered *graven.* In all other places where it is found, Rev. xiii: 16, 17; xiv: 9, 11; xv: 2; xvi: 2; xix: 20; xx: 4, it is rendered 'mark', and is applied to the same thing—the mark of the beast. The word properly means, something graven or sculptured: hence (A,) a graving, sculpture, sculptured work, as images or idols; (B,) a mark cut in or stamped—as the stamp on coin."

We have brought forward Mr. Barnes, as a respectable translator and competent witness, to prove that the word in our translation, rendered "mark," is an engraving or graven mark of the Beast, stamped, cut in, or graven upon the persons of the men who worship the Beast and his Image. The testimony of Barnes in this case is all the more valuable because he himself has found no literal fulfillment of the prophecy he has so clearly described. Barnes has given us the word; let Webster give us the meaning of it. *"Engrave,* To cut with a chisel or graver; to impress deeply.—*Mark,* A significative token."

With what clearness, with what fatal precision does this prophecy point out the engraver's chisel and the working-tools of the stone-masons, used by Freemasons, in the initiation of candidates into the fraternity that worships the Beast. A man who had been initiated, recently told the writer, that his flesh smarted from the heavy pressure of the compasses on his naked breast. The Entered Apprentice and Master Mason are thus marked. The Fellow Craft is received on the angle of the square; and the Mark Master is most fatally marked with the engraver's chisel on the left breast. We will give an exact quotation from Richardson's "Monitor."

"*Senior Deacon*, (approaching candidate with a mallet and engraving-chisel in his hand.) Brother, it becomes my duty to place a mark upon you, which you will probably carry to your grave. As an Entered Apprentice Mason, you were received upon the point of the compasses, pressing your naked left breast; as a Fellow Craft Mason, you were received upon the angle of the square, pressing your naked right breast; as a Master Mason, you were received upon both points of the compasses, extending from your naked left to right breast. They were then explained to you. The chisel and mallet (placing the edge of the chisel against his breast,) are instruments used by Operative Masons to hew, cut, carve and indent their work; but we, as free and accepted Masons, make use of them for a more noble and glorious purpose. We use them to hew, cut, carve and indent the mind; and as a Mark Master Mason, we receive you upon the edge of the indenting chisel, and under the pressure of the mallet. As he pronounces the last words, he braces his feet, raises his mallet and makes two or three false motions, and gives a violent blow upon the head of the chisel."

Careful reader, could God have described these idolatrous marks any plainer than he has done, without so alarming the Freemason that he would refuse to receive them; and by thus interfering with man's free agency, either have rendered the prophecy unnecessary, or defeated its fulfillment?

Freemasons also call the penalty of an obligation, in connection with its sign, "a sign and the mark of a sign," "a penal sign," and "the mark of a sign." A penalty is to have a nail driven into the temple; the sign is to touch the temple with the finger of the right hand. We presume that God, as well as a Freemason, understands this to be another way of marking the forehead and the hand. These marks appertain to the mysteries of the heathen department of the Roman Empire; and being also fundamental to the Lodge, are transfused through every department of the Secret Empire.

The stone-masons and builders of the Roman Empire were called Guilds, Colleges and Corporations, and being incorporated into the civil compact by civil law, were an integrant part of the Empire; and in prophetic style, they constituted a very prominent portion of the Beast. Speculative Freemasons assume their corporate privileges, and retain their working-tools, which they transform into religious symbols, or symbols of the Beast. With these implements, they mark the candidate on his naked person; by these they teach him every duty he is to perform. The following quotations are from Cross's "Masonic Chart:"

"The chisel morally demonstrates the advantages of discipline and education.—The mallet morally teaches to correct irregularities, and reduce man to a proper level.—The trowel is used for the glorious purpose of spreading the cement of brotherly love and affection.—The plumb admonishes us to walk uprightly in our several stations before God and man.—By a due regard to the use of the compasses, the craft is taught to circumscribe their desires and keep their passions within due bounds.—The common gavel is an instrument made use of by operative masons [the Builders of the Empire,] to break off the superfluous corners of rough stones, the better to fit them for the builders' use; but we, as free and accepted Masons, are taught to make use of it, for the more noble and glorious purpose of divesting our hearts and consciences of all the vices and superfluities of life, thereby fitting our minds, as living stones, for that spiritual building, that house not made with hands, eternal in the heavens."

Just as sure as Christ instituted the Lord's Supper; and as the bread and wine employed by His followers as symbols, refer to Christ: so were the corporate Builders an institution of the Beast; and their working-tools, when employed by Freemasons as symbols, refer to the Beast. From these tools as symbols, Freemasons draw their hopes of salvation. And as Christians, in the employment of symbols in the Sacrament, worship Christ; so do Masons, in the employment of their symbols, worship the Beast.

Upon this point, many concentric lines of argument are brought to bear; many truths, like rays of light converging, center here; showing to the careful reader, a conclusion too strong to be false, where facts the most literal and proximate, give to argument its maximum of power; argument which proves beyond the possibility of reasonable doubt, that Freemasonry is THE IMAGE OF THE BEAST; that its marks are the Marks of the Beast; that its worship is the worship of the Beast; and that the Masonic organization is symbolized in the Word of God, and condemned.

# CHAPTER XIII.

It may be a duty which devolves upon us, to say a few words to Freemasons, before we close; especially to the Christian Freemason, so called; though this may seem to many, a contradiction in terms. But a nominal Mason who is, in heart, a Christian, may be ignorant on Masonic questions, while intelligent on others. If the reader should be an intelligent Freemason, and at the same time a professing Christian, we wish to place a few thoughts before him to warn him of the dangers which everywhere surround him; that if we cannot persuade him to leave the Masonic institution forever, our words of admonition may, at least, serve to warn others not to bind their souls with fetters too strong to be broken.

Your standard authorities declare openly and with evident pride, that "the religion of Masonry is pure Theism;" and your authentic Rituals proclaim salvation through the teachings of Masonic symbols. This proves that your "pure Theism" is something infinitely worse than pure Deism.

Your symbols come from the Beast, and refer to the Beast; by them you worship the Beast, and receive the marks of the Beast. Now what is there in the Beast that you, as a Christian, can love? Is not the Beast, according to the Word of God and the history of the world, the dreadful foe of God and Christians?—having trampled fifteen millions of martyrs beneath his feet since the eighth century, besides the countless numbers who fell before his relentless power, in the ten persecutions of earlier times, including the apostles among the number, and even Christ himself, who suffered under Tiberius Cæsar and Pontius Pilate. How can you love those governmental forms so often used to crush the Church of God? How can you delight to wear the badge or costume, or assume the titles of the murderers of your Savior and His people? If you are a Christian, how can you worship the image of all these things in Masonry? In worshiping the power that first killed Christ and then slew His saints, do you not crucify Him again, and put Him to an open shame? Are you not silent while you hear some Masonic Pilate driving down the nails? Do you not dishonor His wounds, and count the blood wherewith you were bought, an unholy thing? When you enter into covenant with the Blue Lodge, not to ask pardon of the Father in His name, do you not thus deny Him and say, "l know not the man?" If you are a Christian, go out of the Lodge quickly, and weep bitterly. Yet rejoice amid your tears, that God did not suffer you to irrecoverably fall into the bottomless Masonic abyss, where deep below deep, extending downward, presents a hollow bosom to the falling soul, which cannot make a lodgment, nor find the lowest deep. Be warned of the danger impending if you remain in the Lodge. Were not Judas and the Man of Sin called the sons of perdition because their perdition and unchangeable doom was certified beforehand? Unless you can answer our arguments, you must admit that the doom of the Lodge is foretold.

*First:*—None of those who have the mark of the Beast are among the saved. "I saw them that had gotten the victory over the Beast, and over his Image, and over his mark, and over the number of his name, stand on the sea of glass, having the harps of God; and they sing the song of Moses the servant of God, and of the Lamb.—And I saw the souls of them that were beheaded for the witness of Jesus, and for the Word of God, and who had not worshiped the Beast, neither his Image, neither had received his mark upon their foreheads nor in their hands; and they lived and reigned with Christ a thousand years."

*Second:*—They are all among the lost. "If any worship the Beast and his Image, and receive his mark in his forehead, or in his hand, the same shall drink of the wine of the wrath of God, which is poured out without without mixture into the cup of His indignation; and he shall be tormented with fire and brimstone, in the presence of the holy angels, and in the presence of the Lamb; and the smoke of their torments ascends up forever and ever and they have no rest day nor night, who worship the Beast and his Image, and whosoever receives the mark of his name."

Such is your appalling state, as seen from a prophetic stand-point. Nor does it relieve the picture to view it from any other position.

Freemasonry is a brotherhood not bounded by any religion or country. Men of various grades of character belong to it. With these, you have entered into a league, offensive and defensive. Masonic law, which demands the life of a seceding Mason, is the bond of union between you. You have all sworn to maintain it under Masonic forms, the strongest known to man, according to Masonic judgment. Your own highest authorities declare that no human power can "cancel your obligations." You have given a mortgage on your interests, and pledged your honor to maintain this law. There are death-penalties lying against your life this moment in one form or another, involving the loss of your heart, brains, or other vital parts, to impel you to commit the sin of maintaining Masonic law, and to remain silent before the civil law, when you know that any of your brethren have committed it, and assist the guilty party as he may need. You are sworn to maintain laws which, you are told, are the same in every nation, and in every age.

Such is the nature of the Masonic compact, that all Freemasons are guilty of the sins of each, and each is guilty of the sins of all. Just as if ten men had sworn to take the life of one, and one of the number should kill him; there would be ten murders committed, one in every heart; and the civil law would hold them all guilty. So it is with the Masonic compact, extending over the world. Are you not a partner to every crime and to every murder resulting from Masonic law, in every age and in every clime, from the blood of the first man who suffered the penalty of Masonic law, to the blood of the last who shall thus suffer death by Masonic hands? The voluntary partnership you have formed and maintain with men of every religion and of no religion, and of every country, makes it possible for you to be a partner to some new murder every day, and very probable that you are. In the same sense, you are also a partner to every other sin committed in the name of Masonry.

You may yet escape this immensity of iniquity, if strong delusion has not so darkened all the approaches to your soul, till already you too firmly believe a lie. If indeed your faith is fixed in falsehood, deep draughts of false morality have made you too drunk to reason and too insensible to feel, Masonic morality, the natural action of which, inverts every principle of the Divine government, and sails things immutable, as though it could interchange the natures of right and wrong in the

Masonic system. It seems to have forced vice and virtue to exchange their places and their names. According to this system, to confess the whole truth in regard to Masonry, is perjury, and repentance unto life, a sin; and that kind of communication which is strictly true to the Lodge, will always be known as a falsehood everywhere else in the universe.

So great is the change produced on the character of men who have become Freemasons, that Masonic authorities call it "regeneration," "new birth," "born again," etc.; and Albert Mackey attaches to these Masonic conversions, the idea of final and certain perseverance. His own language is, "Once a Mason, always a Mason." There is here a frightful harmony between Albert Mackey and the prophecy: "And there fell a noisome and grievous *sore* upon the men who had the mark of the Beast, and upon them that worshiped his Image." Again, they "blasphemed the God of heaven because of their *sores,* and repented not of their deeds." What strength there must be in Freemasonry, that can make men persevere, until their souls are shaken, responsive to the last utterance of the Spirit's voice, "Let us depart?"

Cold will freeze, and heat will burn; their greatest antagonism existing in their greatest extremes. The greatest opposing power will be found to inhere in the greatest extreme from the principle opposed. Everything physical and moral has an opposing power in its opposite extreme. Light has its antagonist in darkness; truth, in error; heaven, in hell. The greatest power for evil exists in an organization where sin stands at its climacteric, unrestrained by any law of God or man. Herein lies the secret of Masonic power to subdue the wills of men, and chain their consciences in cells of moral darkness. Christianity and Masonry are opposite extremes of vast conflicting power, where Christ and Bacchus sit on adverse thrones, both proclaiming salvation to the world; the one, truly and to all mankind, through his own blood; the other, falsely to a favored few, though millions in the aggregate, through Masonic symbols. Christianity is light and truth, courting investigation and hating darkness. Masonry is darkness and falsehood, fleeing from the face of day, and persecuting with relentless hatred those who dare to question its character. It is a hideous moral midnight which, forever retreating from the sun, keeps itself antipodal to noon, where it holds in silence its gloomy, central, solitary reign.

## THE END.

Seal not the sayings of the prophecy of this book, for the time is at hand.—*Rev.* xxii: 10.

www.ingramcontent.com/pod-product-compliance
Lightning Source LLC
Chambersburg PA
CBHW032126160426
43197CB00008B/533